BRITISH HISTORY
The Middle Ages

1154–1485

KINGFISHER

 KINGFISHER

First published in 1992 by Kingfisher
This revised, reformatted and updated
edition published in 2007 by Kingfisher
an imprint of Macmillan Children's Books
20 New Wharf Road, London N1 9RR
Associated companies around the world
www.panmacmillan.com

Consultant: David Haycock

ISBN 978 0 7534 1477 4

This edition copyright © Macmillan Publishers International Ltd 2007

Material in this edition previously published by Kingfisher in the
Children's Illustrated Encyclopedia of British History in 1992

3 5 7 9 8 6 4 2

2SPL/0416/UTD/WKT/115MA

A CIP catalogue record for this book is available from the British Library.

Printed in China

CONTENTS

THE PLANTAGENETS
(1154 – 1399)

THE PLANTAGENETS RULED ENGLAND for almost 250 years. These were years of strife and violence, but they also saw the beginnings of English democracy in the birth of Parliament. It was Plantagenet kings who fought the Hundred Years War against the French, initially winning most of the battles but losing the war and most of England's French possessions. The name Plantagenet was a nickname for the founder of the dynasty, Geoffrey of Anjou, who wore a sprig of broom, *planta genista*, as a badge. But the name does not appear to have been used by the royal family itself until the mid-1400s so some historians prefer to call Henry II and his sons Angevins, men from Anjou.

Geoffrey Plantagenet, Count of Anjou, whose son began 250 years of Plantagenet rule in Britain.

Henry II

HENRY OF ANJOU, the son of Matilda and Geoffrey of Anjou, became Henry II, the first Plantagenet King of England, in 1154. He immediately set about ruthlessly destroying the castles of those barons who had opposed him during Stephen's reign. He also wanted more control over the Church, which had a powerful hold over ordinary people during these times.

THOMAS à BECKET

In 1155 Henry appointed his friend, a priest Thomas à Becket, as Chancellor, the chief minister of England. Later, in 1162, Henry persuaded Becket to become Archbishop of Canterbury. He thought that as both Archbishop and Chancellor Becket would do his bidding and help keep the Church in check. But Becket "put God before the king" and defended the rights and possessions of the Church. Henry set out his Church reforms in the Constitutions of Clarendon in 1164 – including the trial of clergy in the Crown's courts, not the Church's own courts. Becket and Henry were in such bitter conflict that twice Becket had to flee to France. When he returned the second time in 1170, Henry is said to have cried out in anger: "Who will rid me of this turbulent priest?" Four knights took Henry at his word, went to Canterbury and brutally murdered Becket at the foot of the altar steps in the cathedral. This aroused horror in Europe and Becket was made a saint.

Above: **Henry II (1154-1189) was one of the most powerful rulers of the Middle Ages. A man of great humour but violent temper, he brought England a time of peace and prosperity.**

TIME CHART

● **1154** Henry II King of England (to 1189). Henry appoints Thomas à Becket Lord Chancellor

● **1162** Thomas à Becket appointed Archbishop of Canterbury. Henry raises Danegeld for the last time

● **1163** Oxford University established

● **1164** Constitutions of Clarendon: clerics condemned by the Church to be punished by lay courts. Becket goes into exile

● **1170** Henry has his son crowned king to ensure succession. Becket is murdered in Canterbury Cathedral

● **1171** Henry invades Ireland and the Irish princes submit

● **1172** Synod of Cashel: Irish Church reformed along English lines. Henry absolved of murder of Becket

● **1173** Henry's family rebel in France. Barons in England join them. Henry crushes revolt in France and imprisons Queen Eleanor. Becket made a saint

Below: **In 1173 Henry II ruled more of France than the French king, Louis VII.**

Left: **On December 29, 1170, Thomas à Becket was murdered on the steps of the altar of Canterbury Cathedral for having opposed the king. Many miracles were soon reported at his tomb. He was made a saint three years later.**

THE INVASION OF IRELAND

England's long and troubled involvement in Ireland began in the reign of Henry II. Henry took advantage of the fact that Irish clan chiefs were fighting each other to claim the title of *Ard-Rí*, or High King. In 1166 he sent a force led by Richard de Clare, Earl of Pembroke, who was also known as Strongbow, to support the King of Leinster in Ireland. In 1171 Strongbow invaded Ireland, claiming the authority of the Pope to convert the Irish Celtic Church to the Roman Church. Irish kings, nobles and bishops submitted to his forces in the same year.

HENRY II'S SONS

Henry II had four strong-willed and unruly sons: Henry, Richard, Geoffrey and John. Henry, the eldest, was known as the Young King because his father had him crowned during his own lifetime to protect the succession. Henry II gave each of his three elder sons lands from his French possessions: the Young King had Normandy, Maine and Anjou; Richard had Aquitaine; Geoffrey had Brittany; but John received no territories to rule and so people at the time nicknamed him Lackland.

The four sons were encouraged by their mother Eleanor, to rebel against the king. She had already fallen out with Henry II in an unhappy marriage. Henry and Geoffrey both died before their father. Henry II fought against Richard and John and kept Eleanor imprisoned for much of their married life. Henry's sons never succeeded in overthrowing him.

THE CRUSADES

Since the Norman times, Anglo-Norman knights had become involved in the crusades. The crusades were a series of military expeditions undertaken by European Christians over 3,000 kilometres away in the Middle East. Their aim was to recover the Holy Lands, where Christianity began, from Muslim occupation. There were eight major crusades from 1095 to 1270, most of which were failures, though a Christian kingdom of Jerusalem was briefly established. During the Middle Ages, many men and women made journeys, called pilgrimages, to Jerusalem and other holy places in Palestine where Jesus had lived and died.

Left: **The Archbishop of Canterbury is the head of the Church of England. The first archbishop was St Augustine, who founded an abbey in Canterbury in 597. Archbishop Lanfranc laid the foundations for the Cathedral from 1070-1089. Thomas à Becket was murdered in the cathedral in 1170 and his tomb there became a centre of pilgrimage.**

FOCUS ON A MEDIEVAL MARKET

Most medieval towns had fairs and markets. Markets were usually held once a week, when farmers from local villages would bring their produce and livestock to sell. There were stalls for butter, salt and fish, as well as shops selling pies for a penny. Metal, leather and woodwork would also be for sale. Beggars and pick-pockets mingled with the crowds looking at the many craft and food stalls while jugglers, musicians and dancing bears entertained passers-by. This picture shows the stone, 14th century Market Cross in Chichester, in West Sussex.

Official business would be done in the market hall at the centre of the square. Many such halls survive today, for example, in Chipping Campden in Gloucestershire and Chipping Norton in Oxfordshire (chipping means selling). Some larger medieval towns had annual fairs where merchants and traders from other parts of the country and overseas exchanged goods. St Giles Fair, held in Oxford, dates back to medieval times.

Richard I and the Crusades

THE CHRISTIAN CHURCH had lost control of the Holy Lands to the Arabs in the 7th century. The Arabs were Muslims and followed Mohammed, founder of the religion of Islam. At first they let Christian pilgrims visit the holy places. But when Muslim Turks invaded the region they began to attack the Christian pilgrims.

In 1095 Pope Urban II called on Christians to liberate Jerusalem from the Turks. Up to 25,000 people, from knights to paupers, travelled to Constantinople, and went on to capture Jerusalem in 1099 in the First Crusade.

Above: **A knight of the crusades.**

A famous legend tells of Blondel, a minstrel who tirelessly searched for, and found, the lost king. Richard was rescued only when his long-suffering subjects paid an enormous ransom – but they warmly welcomed him back to London. Soon, however, he left for Normandy to defend his French lands. Richard was mortally wounded by an archer while

Right: **Saladin, the great Muslim general and sultan of the Saracens. He united the Muslim kingdoms and from 1187 led them in a** *jihad* **(holy war) against the Christian crusaders – among them Richard the Lionheart, King of England.**

THE THIRD CRUSADE

Nearly 100 years later English knights were among the main participants in the Third Crusade. The great Muslim leader, Saladin, had recaptured Jerusalem from the crusaders in 1187. Richard I came to the throne in 1189 as a soldier already admired for his skill and courage. His bravery earned him the name *Coeur de Lion*, the Lionheart.

That year Richard responded to the Pope's call to try to win Jerusalem back from the Muslim Turks. He came within sight of Jerusalem, but never recaptured it from the Muslims. He did, however, secure a five-year peace treaty with Saladin. This allowed European pilgrims to visit the holy places again. During negotiations, Saladin sent Richard, who had become ill, fresh fruit and snow water to help him recover.

RICHARD: THE ABSENT KING

On his way home from the Holy Lands, Richard was captured, handed over to his enemy, the Holy Roman Emperor Henry VI, and held prisoner.

Left: **Richard I, (on the right) wearing the red cross of the crusaders. He led an army of knights to the Holy Land in 1189 on the Third Crusade.**

besieging the castle of Chaluz, in France, in 1199. Richard spent only seven months of his ten-year reign in Britain – and that was to raise money for the Third Crusade by selling Church and state lands and charters of self-government to the towns.

IMPACT OF THE CRUSADES

The crusades may have been a military failure for Europe, but returning crusaders brought back with them valuable spices, such as nutmeg and cinnamon, along with sugar, cotton and Oriental tapestries. They also brought back Arabic ideas about science, medicine, philosophy and art.

Below: **A battle between Muslims and Christian knights. The crusaders sewed big crosses onto their clothes, having taken up the call of the Pope to "wear Christ's cross as your badge. If you are killed your sins will be pardoned". Some knights who were also monks formed a full-time regiment in Jerusalem called the Knights of St John, or the Knights Hospitallers.**

- **1174** Henry II does penance at Canterbury for Becket's murder. William of Scotland invades Northumberland and is captured. Henry crushes English revolt and makes peace with his sons. Treaty of Falaise: William of Scotland freed after paying homage to Henry

- **1176** Assize of Northampton: Henry establishes judicial rules. Eisteddfod held at Cardigan

- **1178** Henry establishes Central Court of Justice

- **1179** Grand Assize of Windsor curbs power of feudal courts

- **1180** Wells Cathedral begun

- **1186** Henry makes peace with Philip II of France

- **1187** Henry and Philip of France agree to go on the Third Crusade

- **1188** Richard, third son of Henry, does homage to Philip II

- **1189** Philip and Richard force Henry to acknowledge Richard as heir. Death of Henry: Richard I succeeds him (to 1199). Massacre of Jews at Richard's coronation

- **1189-1192** Richard and Philip of France lead Third Crusade but fail to take Jerusalem

- **1191** Civil war in England between Richard's brother John and William Longchamp

- **1192** Leopold of Austria captures Richard as he travels to England

- **1193** John claims the throne

- **1194** Richard is freed and returns to England; John flees to France

- **1199** Richard killed at siege of Chaluz; John succeeds him (to 1216)

The Magna Carta

KING JOHN, RICHARD'S BROTHER, was a tough, energetic man. Like many other Plantagenets, he was given to violent rages and cruelty. One of his early acts as king was to order the murder of his nephew, Arthur, whom he had imprisoned at Rouen in France. This young prince, as son of John's older brother Geoffrey, had a good claim to the throne.

Arthur's murder and John's behaviour provoked the barons of Anjou and Poitou into fighting against John. He lost most of his French lands and also angered the Pope by refusing to accept his choice of Archbishop of Canterbury. When John took the clergy's lands, Pope Innocent III banned nearly all Church services in England.

KING JOHN AGAINST THE BARONS

John continued to confiscate Church property, so in 1213 the Pope declared that John was no longer the rightful king of England, and granted Philip of France the right to depose him. As John had already angered his English barons by taxing them harshly and abusing feudal rights, it was not long before the English barons joined forces and rebelled against the king.

In June 1215 John was forced to meet the barons in a meadow beside the River Thames at Runnymede. There John put his seal to a document the barons had drawn up to confirm their rights against the king. This document was the famous Magna Carta, or Great Charter. It established certain curbs on royal abuses of power and laid the foundation for British democracy.

Above: **The Children's Crusade in 1212 involved possibly up to 50,000 French and German children who tried to reach the Holy Land. Most were turned back or were sold as slaves.**

- **1201** John grants a charter to Jews

- **1203** Arthur of Brittany, John's nephew, murdered

- **1204** Philip of France conquers Normandy from John

- **1205** Dispute over new Archbishop of Canterbury: John nominates John de Grey, Bishop of Norwich

- **1206** Pope Innocent III rejects de Grey's nomination, supports election of Stephen Langton as Archbishop of Canterbury

- **1207** John rejects Langton. Port of Liverpool founded

- **1208** Pope puts England under interdict, or exclusion. Llewelyn the Great seizes Powys

Below: **The English succession. Claimants to the Crown are underlined.**

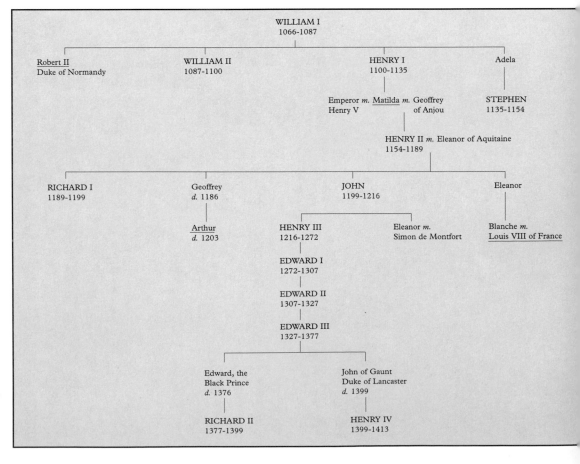

WHAT THE CHARTER SET OUT

Four original copies of the Magna Carta exist, one each in Lincoln and Salisbury Cathedrals and two in the British Museum. Most of the 63 clauses in the Magna Carta pledged the king to upholding the feudal system of the barons, but some also protected the rights of freemen, those citizens not tied to feudal lords. Clauses which have had great influence included the following: in all important matters the king must seek the barons' advice; no special taxes could be raised without the barons' consent; no freeman (those not tied to feudal lords) should be imprisoned or exiled, or deprived of property, except by the law of the land; and (one of the most important clauses) "to none will we sell, to none will we deny or delay right of justice". This ensured the basic right of free justice for all regardless of the seriousness of the crime or the individual's wealth or position.

After all the trouble with Rome, the Church was to be formally guaranteed certain long sought-after rights including freedom from state control, and the right to elect archbishops, bishops, abbots and other senior Church representatives.

EFFECT OF THE CHARTER

The effect of the Charter was that the king could continue to rule, but must keep to the laws of the land, and could be forced to do so. The Magna Carta was in force for only a few weeks before John persuaded the Pope to revoke it. Civil war broke out and John died in 1216. The Magna Carta was reissued in a revised form and, in 1225, became the law of the land.

Above: **King John's great seal which was attached to the Magna Carta. It showed the King's agreement so turning the Charter into law.**

Right: **A page from the Magna Carta. There are four copies of the Magna Carta: one each in Lincoln and Salisbury Cathedrals, and two in the British Museum.**

- **1209** London Bridge completed (stands until 1832). Some scholars leave Oxford for Cambridge (the beginning of Cambridge University)

- **1213** Philip II of France accepts Pope's mandate to conquer England. John accepts Langton as Archbishop of Canterbury; papal interdict is lifted. English ships destroy French fleet

- **1214** French defeat English and allies at battle of Bouvines. Barons threaten revolt. John takes crusader vows, and in return Pope excommunicates the barons

- **1215** John agrees to Magna Carta. Pope annuls Magna Carta; civil war resumes

- **1216** Louis of France invades England. John dies: succeeded by son Henry III, aged 9 (to 1272). William Marshal becomes regent. Magna Carta reissued

- **1217** William Marshal defeats the French at the battle of Lincoln; French leave England

Rivals for the Throne

Henry III CAME TO THE THRONE aged only nine as John's eldest son. In his youth the country was well governed for him by William Marshal, Earl of Pembroke, and then by Hubert de Burgh, who was the Justiciar. When he grew up Henry III came under the influence of foreign barons and courtiers: first Peter des Roches from Poitou, Bishop of Winchester, and then des Roches' nephew (or perhaps son), Peter des Rivaux. Henry married Eleanor of Provence in 1236, and her many uncles from Savoy were given large estates and positions of power. Chief among them was Peter of Savoy, to whom Henry gave an estate near London, by the Thames; the Savoy Hotel and Theatre now stand on this site.

Although Henry III was a pious, sensitive man, he was completely without any ability to govern by himself. His inept and spendthrift ways upset the English nobles (those original Norman barons who came to England during the Norman Conquest).

SIMON DE MONTFORT

One of these nobles was Simon de Montfort, who came to England in 1229 to claim the earldom of Leicester, which he inherited through his grandmother. De Montfort quickly became a favourite of Henry, and of the king's sister Eleanor, whom he married. Henry's misrule and his reliance on foreigners made the barons take up arms against him. They assembled a Great Council in Oxford in 1258, and with de Montfort as their leader they forced the king to swear to the Provisions of Oxford, in return for financial help to cover his debts. These Provisions said that the king was to rule with the advice of a council of barons.

WELSH RESISTANCE

The conquest of Wales was carried out by powerful barons known as the Lords Marchers, because they guarded the marches, or frontiers, between Wales and England. The wild northern regions of Wales remained largely independent and it was in North Wales at this time that the Welsh archers developed the longbow, which became one of the most formidable weapons of its day.

Above: **Henry III (1216-1272) became king at the age of nine but did not rule until 1234. Simon de Montfort and the English barons rebelled against his favouritism and promotion of foreign men at Court.**

Below: **English bases in North Wales. Massive castles were built at key sites to control the Welsh.**

Above: **Simon de Montfort, leader of the dissatisfied barons, as shown in a window of Chartres Cathedral.**

Below: **Caernarfon Castle was built as a royal residence. The Eagle Tower is about 22 metres in diameter. The central gate had five double doors.**

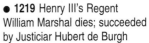

● **1219** Henry III's Regent William Marshal dies; succeeded by Justiciar Hubert de Burgh

● **1224** The king recovers royal castles held by the barons. Louis VIII of France declares war

● **1225** Henry reissues Magna Carta and Charter of the Forests, in return for grant of general tax

● **1227** Henry declares himself to be of age to rule; but Hubert de Burgh retains power

● **1228** Death of Stephen Langton. Llewelyn the Great besieges Montgomery; Henry relieves city. Sixth Crusade: Jerusalem taken

● **1229** Llewelyn nominates his son David as his successor. Henry tries to take an army to France to recover his lands, but de Burgh fails to provide shipping

● **1230** Henry's French campaign fails

● **1231** England and France make a truce

● **1232** Henry dismisses de Burgh. Peter des Roches, Bishop of Winchester, becomes adviser to the king

Above: **Two knights fight each other in a mock battle, or joust, at a tournament. Each knight had his coat-of-arms on his shield, on the crest of his helmet and on his horse's trappings.**

LLEWELYN THE GREAT

One of the leading princes of Wales in the early 13th century was Llewelyn the Great, prince of Gwynedd in North Wales. Llewelyn was also accepted as leader by the people of South Wales. In the early part of the reign of Henry III, Llewelyn was driven back from South Wales by the Regent, William Marshal, Earl of Pembroke. But Llewelyn increased his territory to include Gwynedd, Clwyd, Powys and part of Dyfed. His younger son, David, became Prince of Gwynedd from 1240 to 1246.

Below: **Longbow archers prepare to fire their arrows. A good archer could shoot ten arrows a minute accurately over a distance of 180 metres.**

9

LLEWELYN THE LAST

In 1246 the throne passed to David's nephews Llewelyn ap Gruffydd (the Last) and his brother Owen. Threatened by claims on Wales from Henry III and others, the brothers united and fought with such determination that, by the Peace of Woodstock in 1247, Henry was forced to recognize them as rightful rulers, so long as they paid homage to him. Llewelyn later declared himself Prince of Wales, up to that time the English had only known him as Lord of Snowdon. In 1282 he died in a rebellion against Edward I and earned the title Llewelyn the Last.

DE MONTFORT RULES ENGLAND

In 1261 Henry persuaded the Pope to absolve him from his oath under the Provisions of Oxford, and won over many barons who now disliked de Montfort's high-handed ways. De Montfort, who had gone abroad, returned to lead a rebellion which restored the Provisions of Oxford. Louis IX of France was then asked to act as judge, and decided in Henry's favour. At this, de Montfort resorted to arms, and in 1264 defeated and captured Henry III at the battle of Lewes, on the Sussex Downs. De Montfort ruled England in the king's name and summoned a parliament which gave the barons greater control over the king.

THE BEGINNINGS OF PARLIAMENT

The term parliament comes from the French word *parleyment*, or talking place. Parliament as a royal council of the English kings came into existence during the reign of Henry III. But the idea of a king's council went back to the Anglo-Saxon Witan, and later the *Curia Regis*, or King's Council, of the Norman king, Henry I. The king usually only called the council when he wanted loans or advice. It was made up of bishops and nobles who held land granted to them by the king.

Simon de Montfort's Parliament was different because when he called an assembly (with the king still as prisoner) in 1265 he did not invite just the barons. He also summoned the elected representatives of the counties, called knights of the shire, and two burgesses from each city or large town. For the first time ever, all classes of people were included, except villeins and serfs.

Left: Edward I (1272-1307) was nicknamed "Longshanks" because he was very tall and had long arms and legs. He was a skilful general and a strong and respected leader. He was also devoted to his queen, Eleanor.

This was to become the beginning of a separate council from the king's council of lords – the House of Commons. The first Act of Parliament to be recorded was the Statute of Merton in 1275. It allowed landlords to enclose common land and also declared that children born out of marriage were considered illegitimate.

While Parliament was meeting, some barons quarrelled with de Monfort, and Henry III's son, Edward, defeated and killed de Montfort at the battle of Evesham in 1265. During his lifetime de Montfort was so popular with the English people that he was known as Good Sir Simon. Henry III took control of the kingdom again until his death in 1272.

EDWARD I: THE LAWGIVER

Edward I, who was 33 when he came to the throne in 1272, was brisk, capable, and an experienced general. His love of order led him to reform the government.

The many laws passed in Edward's reign have earned him the nickname of the Lawgiver. He was the first English king to use Parliament as an instrument of government to reform the law of the land. Among his early reforms were three Statutes of Westminster, all of which dealt with local government and the ownership and inheritance of land. The Statute of Wales marked the end of Wales as a separate country; but left Welsh common law, language and customs intact. Edward also built impressive castles in North Wales from 1283 to 1307, including Caernarfon which is still standing today.

Below: **The Middle Ages, or medieval period as it is also known, was a time of wars across the borders in Scotland and Wales, and violence in England with barons struggling against the king and against each other. Castles were built and walled towns had to be well guarded with soldiers on sentry duty day and night.**

● **1233** Revolt of Richard Marshal, Earl of Pembroke, allied with Llewelyn. Richard defeats royal forces near Monmouth

● **1234** Henry III makes peace with Richard. Richard murdered in Ireland

● **1237** Barons insist on nominating three of Henry's counsellors

● **1240** Llewelyn the Great dies; succeeded by son David (to 1246)

● **1241** Henry leads expedition to Wales. Peter of Savoy, uncle of Queen Eleanor is royal adviser

● **1242** Henry defeated by Louis IX of France. Barons refuse to pay for French war

● **1245** Building of Westminster Abbey is begun

● **1246** Welsh prince David dies; succeeded by Llewelyn the Last (to 1282) and his brother Owen

● **1257** Llewelyn assumes the title Prince of Wales

● **1258** Provisions of Oxford: barons take control of Henry's government

● **1261** Pope absolves Henry from the oath to observe the Provisions of Oxford

● **1262** Llewelyn attacks England

● **1263** Simon de Montfort returns as leader of the barons; Henry accepts the barons' terms

● **1264** Battle of Lewes: de Montfort defeats and captures Henry

● **1265** De Montfort's Parliament. Battle of Evesham: Henry's son Edward defeats and kills de Montfort

● **1266** Roger Bacon invents the magnifying glass

● **1267** Henry recognizes Llewelyn as Prince of Wales

WAR WITH SCOTLAND

In Scotland, the barons asked Edward to choose a successor to Alexander III, Edward's brother-in-law, who had died without an heir in 1286. Edward I selected John Balliol as ruler of Scotland but treated him as a puppet king. The barons rebelled and in 1296 Edward invaded Scotland and captured Balliol. For ten years after this Scotland was without a king. Edward tried to rule it himself, but he was defied by William Wallace, who led an uprising and made himself master of Scotland. Wallace was an extraordinary general who managed to inspire half-armed peasant foot soldiers to take on the might of mail-clad knights. However, Edward reconquered the country and captured Wallace, who was put to death in 1305.

ROBERT BRUCE AND BANNOCKBURN

Within months of William Wallace's death, Robert Bruce became the great champion of Scotland. He was crowned King of Scotland at Scone in 1306, but an English army was quickly on the scene and Bruce suffered two heavy defeats. After a spell in hiding, Bruce defeated an English army twice as strong as his own at the battle of Bannockburn in 1314. This battle ensured that Scotland would stay independent of England.

In 1320 at the abbey of Arbroath, in Angus, an assembly of Scottish lords drew up a declaration of independence. It affirmed loyalty to Robert Bruce. Edward II agreed to a truce with Scotland. First the Treaty of Northampton brought peace to the two countries of England and Scotland. Then the Treaty of Brigham conceded to the Scots that the laws of Scotland were to be respected as independent of those of England. It also confirmed that Scotland itself was to be independent of England, with a distinct border, and that no Scottish subject could be forced to attend an English court.

EDWARD II

The first Prince of Wales became King Edward II in 1307. He was the fourth son of Edward I but his older brothers had all died when he was a boy. Edward therefore relied very much on his friends and favourites, and they in turn influenced his decisions in matters of state, to the fury of the barons. Edward's favourites included Piers Gaveston, whom a group of lords seized and beheaded in 1312. Later, Edward became fiercely loyal to Hugh Despenser and his son, also named Hugh. When the younger Hugh married Edward's cousin, the barons rebelled.

EDWARD III

Edward was only 14 years old when he came to the throne of England. His mother, Isabella of France, and her lover, Roger Mortimer, Earl of March, had ordered Edward II's murder in 1327, and had secured Edward III's succession with Parliament's support. For three years real power lay with this couple. But in 1330 Edward III rebelled against them and took charge of the government.

Right: **Springtime sowing in the countryside in the mid-1300s. Although this was a period marked by royal murders and fighting between barons, as well as war in France, ordinary people got on with their lives. All but 10 percent of the population lived and worked on the land. The earth was ploughed in rough strips from March onwards. The sower scattered the seeds by hand in the furrows of the ploughed ground, not stopping to cover it. Bird scarers used slings and other distractions to stop birds from taking the seeds. The summer months were for haymaking, and the corn was harvested in early September. From 1350 the Black Death was to cut the work force by more than one third.**

Above: The battle of Bannockburn in 1314 was a humiliating defeat for the English and a triumph for Robert Bruce. After eight years of war with England, he finally became the undisputed King of Scotland. It is said that when in hiding, he found the courage to fight on from watching a spider trying again and again to climb its web.

THE HUNDRED YEARS WAR BEGINS

The Hundred Years War between England and France was a series of wars, interspersed with truces. Edward III started the war in 1337, when Charles IV of France died without a direct heir. Edward wanted to secure his claim to the French throne through his mother, Isabella of France. Philip of Valois, who took the French throne, was anxious to regain Gascony, the last major English territory in France. Edward was spurred on by the ideas of chivalry and honour and also knew that if he could unite his restless barons in an overseas quest for honour they were less likely to start trouble at home.

- **1269** Prince Edward goes on crusade. First toll roads in England

- **1272** Henry III dies: Edward I, though absent, proclaimed king (to 1307)

- **1274** Edward I arrives in England and is crowned king. Llewelyn the Last refuses to take oath of allegiance to Edward

- **1275** Edward holds his first Parliament. First Statute of Westminster; wool duties granted to the Crown

- **1277** Edward begins campaign in Wales against Llewelyn, who submits with Treaty of Conway

- **1282** Llewelyn's brother, David, begins a revolt against the English. Edward marches into Wales. Llewelyn killed in battle

- **1283** Welsh revolt collapses. David is executed. Edward begins building castles in Wales

- **1284** Statute of Wales, Welsh government organized

- **1291** Scots ask Edward to choose between 13 claimants to the Scottish throne

- **1292** Edward awards Scottish throne to John Balliol (to 1296), making Scotland a fief of England

- **1296** Edward invades Scotland (Balliol abdicates) and declares himself King of Scotland

- **1297** Wallace leads revolt in Scotland

- **1298** Edward defeats Wallace at Falkirk

- **1301** Edward makes his son, Edward, Prince of Wales

- **1305** Wallace executed

- **1306** Robert Bruce claims Scottish throne (to 1329)

- **1307** Death of Edward. Succeeded by son Edward II (to 1327). Bruce defeats English

Right: The Hundred Years War was not one long war but a series of short ones. It began in 1337 and ended in 1453 (actually 116 years). English longbowmen and pikemen fought French knights on horseback and crossbowmen. Knights who were given land in feudal times had to raise and equip an army if needed. Knights wore heavy armour and rode horses. Foot soldiers wore helmets and tunics.

FOCUS ON THE ORDER OF THE GARTER
Edward III founded the Order of the Garter in 1349 to carry on the medieval ideals of knighthood and chivalry. Legend has it that a countess accidentally dropped her garter while dancing with Edward III. The King picked it up and rebuked his sniggering courtiers with the quip *Honi soit qui mal y pense* (French for *Warning be to him who thinks ill of this*). This is now the motto of the Order. The garter is the highest order of knighthood.

EDWARD'S VICTORIES

Another cause of the Hundred Years War was the wool trade. The weavers of Flanders depended on English wool, and England's wool was their only source of income apart from farming. But the aristocratic rulers of Flanders were pro-French and attempted to curb the English wool trade. Edward III made a treaty with the Flemish weavers in 1338 to reinforce his claims against Philip VI who had already seized Gascony.

In the early years of the war the English won two major battles. The naval battle of Sluys in 1340 gave them control of the English Channel, and made an English invasion of France relatively easy. When the invasion began Edward had a major land victory at Crécy in 1346, on the banks of the Somme. This battle was won by Edward's longbowmen, whose arrows mowed down the French.

THE BLACK DEATH

During Edward III's reign, the greatest disaster befell Europe. In only twenty years the Black Death (bubonic plague carried by rats from Asia) killed about one third of Europe's population. The disease got its name from the spots of blood that formed under the skin and turned black.

The Black Death came to England in 1348, through Melcombe Regis, the port of Weymouth. Within a few weeks it had spread to London and Bristol, where at one stage the living were hardly able to bury the dead. Within a year almost every part of England and Wales had been affected. The death toll was half the country's population at that time.

- **1308** Edward II marries Isabella of France

- **1311** Privy Seal office is established

- **1314** Scots defeat English at the battle of Bannockburn

- **1320** Declaration of Arbroath: Scots lords state to the Pope their loyalty to Robert I (the Bruce)

- **1323** Edward and Robert agree truce

- **1324** French invade Gascony

- **1327** Edward deposed and; Edward III becomes king (to 1377). England regains Gascony

Below: Black rats on board merchant ships carried the bubonic plague in their blood and their fleas transmitted it to people.

Left: European streets in the Middle Ages were filthy places. Open sewers ran down the middle and there were rats and rubbish everywhere. Human waste was thrown out of windows with a cry of "*Gardez-loo*" to warn passers by to get out of the way. Disease spread because of dirt and rats.

- **1328** Edward III makes peace with Scotland. Philip VI becomes the first Valois King of France

- **1330** Edward arrests Roger Mortimer, Earl of March, and begins personal rule

- **1336** Trade with Flanders is halted. French attack Isle of Wight and Channel Islands

- **1337** Philip VI seizes Gascony: start of Hundred Years War. Edward claims French Crown

- **1338** French fleet sacks Portsmouth. Edward lands at Antwerp: makes alliance with German emperor. Flemish weavers make trade treaty with England

- **1340** English naval victory at Sluys wins control of English Channel. Parliament appoints auditors of the king's expenditure

- **1343** France and England make truce

- **1346** Edward defeats French at Crécy

- **1347** Edward captures French port of Calais

- **1348** Black Death reaches England. Edward founds the Order of the Garter

- **1350** Black Death reaches Scotland. Extension of Windsor Castle begins

- **1351** Statute of Labourers curbs wages

Below: The effigy of the Black Prince that lies on top of his tomb in Canterbury Cathedral. He was a brilliant general. During the last years of his life illness made him bedridden and unable to control his armies.

Many villages were abandoned because of the plague. One of these deserted villages has been reconstructed by archaeologists at Cosmeston, near Penarth in South Wales.

The Black Death also halted Edward III's campaign against Scotland, but Scottish rejoicing at this was soon dashed when the plague struck there too. Scotland, Ireland and Wales, however, suffered less severely than England. The Black Death lasted on and off for over 150 years.

THE BLACK PRINCE

Edward III's eldest son, Edward, Prince of Wales, was as fine a soldier as his father, and is known as the Black Prince because of the colour of his armour. In 1346 he distinguished himself by his bravery at the battle of Crécy when he was only 16. The French may have lost over 10,000 men against less than 200 English deaths. Here he won the three plumes and the motto *Ich dien* (German for *I serve*) used by princes of Wales ever since. A truce was made in 1348 but Philip VI died in 1350 and Edward attacked France again.

In 1356 Edward the Black Prince won his greatest victory as a commander at Poitiers, where he captured the French king, John II. This monarch was ransomed for 3 million gold crowns and the Duchy of Aquitaine. While fighting in Spain the Black Prince caught an infection which made him ill and he died in 1376, one year before his father.

Richard II

When Richard succeeded Edward III he was only ten years old and inherited the cost of the Hundred Years War which left the Crown deeply in debt. Richard II was too young to rule, so the country was governed for a decade by his uncles: John, Duke of Lancaster, generally known as John of Gaunt, and Thomas of Gloucester. Their rule was not popular and the introduction of heavy taxes led to the Peasants' Revolt in 1381.

LABOUR UNREST

The immediate effect of the Black Death had been a loss of a third of the labour force, and a rise in workers' wages which amounted to about 50 percent for craftworkers and agricultural workers, and 100 percent for women farm workers. Employers had little choice but to pay, but a Statute of Labourers in 1351 fixed the price of labour to be on the same scale as it had been before the Black Death. Labourers resented this law. The Statute was a failure.

Above: **Richard II (1377-1399) was a lover of art, not of warfare, and suffered from being unfairly compared with his father, the Black Prince, who was a great soldier.**

Below: **Richard II met with the rebels at Smithfield during the Peasants' Revolt in 1381.**

- **1353** Edward III transfers the wool staple (market) from Bruges in Flanders to England

- **1356** Edward Balliol gives up throne of Scotland to Edward. Black Prince defeats and captures John II of France at Poitiers

- **1357** Treaty of Bordeaux between England and France

- **1360** France cedes Aquitaine, Ponthieu and Calais

- **1363** Statute of Apparel prevents people wearing dress above their station in life

- **1364** Hostage for payment of John II's ransom escapes: John returns to captivity, and dies

- **1366** Statutes of Kilkenny: Irish Parliament forbids the English overlords to marry the Irish and bans Irish language, laws and customs

- **1375** Peace with France: England left with only Calais, Brest, Bordeaux and Bayonne. Robin Hood appears in ballads

- **1376** The Good Parliament: first to elect a Speaker. Black Prince dies

- **1377** Edward dies: succeeded by 10-year-old Richard II (to 1399); regency council rules

- **1380** Wyclif translates Bible

- **1381** Peasants' Revolt

- **1387** Geoffrey Chaucer starts The Canterbury Tales

- **1388** Lords Appellant control government

- **1389** Richard II assumes rule

- **1393** Great Statute of Praemunire reasserts supremacy of State in Church affairs

- **1395** Irish chiefs submit to Richard

THE PEASANTS' REVOLT

The Peasants' Revolt of 1381 was led by Wat Tyler, a tiler (though some say a blacksmith), and Jack Straw (possibly a nickname). This open rebellion was sparked off by the imposition of a poll tax of one shilling per head.

More than 20,000 peasants from Kent and Essex marched on London. Here they killed the Archbishop of Canterbury who was also the Chancellor, whom they blamed for imposing the unfair taxes. They also burned John of Gaunt's palace, the Savoy. Richard II, still only 14 years old, faced a mob at Mile End and promised: "You shall have from me all you seek." Tyler and his men of Kent remained armed while the rest dispersed. A few days later, in the king's presence, Tyler was killed by the Lord Mayor of London, William Walworth.

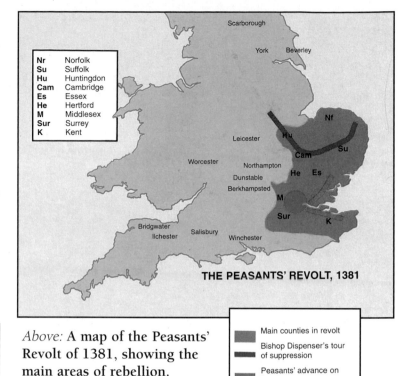

Nr	Norfolk
Su	Suffolk
Hu	Huntingdon
Cam	Cambridge
Es	Essex
He	Hertford
M	Middlesex
Sur	Surrey
K	Kent

THE PEASANTS' REVOLT, 1381

Above: **A map of the Peasants' Revolt of 1381, showing the main areas of rebellion.**

Main counties in revolt

Bishop Dispenser's tour of suppression

Peasants' advance on London

FOCUS ON GEOFFREY CHAUCER

The poet Geoffrey Chaucer was born around 1340 and was squire to Edward III. He travelled to Italy on the king's business where he read books by Dante and Boccaccio. Chaucer wrote for Richard II's court, but his poems were read by a wider audience and were very popular. The most famous is a long poem called *The Canterbury Tales* which follows a group of pilgrims (some shown here) who tell each other stories on the way to Becket's shrine at Canterbury. It was the first important book written in English rather than Latin.

The Miller

The Prioress

The Knight

RICHARD II LOSES CONTROL

When the king's uncle John of Gaunt went off to Spain to pursue a claim to the throne of Castile, there was armed conflict between the king's men and the Duke of Gloucester who, in 1387, had set up a ruling council known as the Lords Appellant. In 1389, Richard took control of the government from the Duke of Gloucester, declaring "I am now old enough to manage my own affairs". For eight years the king's rule was peaceful and prosperous.

But when Richard's wife, Anne of Bohemia, died of the plague in 1394 he was left heartbroken and without purpose.

Richard turned into a tyrant, revenging himself in 1397 on the Lords Appellant. The Earl of Arundel was beheaded. The Duke of Gloucester, Richard's uncle, was murdered. Two others, Henry of Bolingbroke and the Duke of Norfolk, who had quarrelled, were banished. Soon afterwards John of Gaunt died, and Richard seized his estates. This was too much for John's son Henry of Bolingbroke. He returned from exile, swiftly gathered a large body of supporters, defeated the king's forces and took Richard prisoner to the Tower of London. By general consent Richard was deposed, and Henry succeeded to the throne as Henry IV in 1399.

Henry V (1413-1422) was a great soldier who won a famous victory over the French at Agincourt in 1415.

LANCASTER AND YORK

(1399 – 1485)

THE PLANTAGENETS were a fierce and quarrelsome family, and never more so than when disputing the right to the throne. Henry of Lancaster, son of John of Gaunt and grandson of Edward III, battled hard to become Henry IV, the first of the Lancastrian kings.

Much of Henry V's short reign was spent across the English Channel pursuing claims to France (England still held Calais and parts of Bordeaux) in the final stages of the Hundred Years War.

A complicated series of local civil wars involving various noble families who claimed the Crown marked the reign of Henry VI. A strong claim was put forward by Richard, Duke of York. The fighting that followed became known as the Wars of the Roses, from the red and white roses on the badges of the two conflicting families, Lancaster and York. In the end Henry Tudor, great-great-grandson of John of Gaunt, won the throne.

Scotland saw its throne pass to the Stewarts, a gallant and ill-fated family. Wales lost its independence and was gradually integrated with England, while the long struggle by the English to conquer Ireland continued.

Henry IV

HENRY IV had to struggle to hold the Crown, which he had seized by force. In 1400, a rising of Richard II's supporters was quickly crushed. Then Richard died in prison, probably murdered. But this was only the start of Henry's troubles. For the next five years, he had to face one rebellion after another.

THE LOLLARDS

In the late 1300s a religious movement had started in England which attacked many of the beliefs and practices of the Church of Rome. Its followers were known as Lollards, from a Flemish word meaning mutterer. They originally followed the teachings of John Wyclif, but later became more extreme. The Church saw them as heretics, and opponents of the established order of government.

To combat Lollardy, Henry IV's Parliament passed the cruel law *De Heretico Comburendo* (1401), which condemned heretics to suffer death by burning. Henry IV was the first English king to put men to death for their religious beliefs. Many followers of John Wyclif were burned at the stake.

OWEN GLENDOWER

Owen Glendower was the last independent Prince of Wales who ruled lands in North Wales. A feud with his neighbour, Lord Grey de Ruthyn, led to rebellion against England. Henry IV declared Glendower's lands forfeit, and gave them to Grey. Glendower raised an army and the Welsh backed him in what became, from 1402 to 1413, a national rebellion.

Above: **Henry IV (1399-1413) was the first British king whose native language was English. He spent much of his reign fighting rebellions, as well as a major national uprising in Wales.**

Right: **A breech-loading cannon of the 15th century. This cast bronze weapon fired solid balls which could knock down the thickest castle walls. Early cannons were not accurate and sometimes killed their loaders. The use of artillery (firearms) in battle and siege spread quickly throughout Europe. But English forces still relied on their longbowmen and knights on horseback to gain victory as at the battle of Agincourt in 1415.**

- **1399** Henry Bolingbroke seizes the throne as Henry IV

- **1400** Conspiracy by Earls of Huntingdon, Kent and Salisbury to kill Henry fails. Richard II dies in captivity. Henry campaigns in Scotland. Owen Glendower rebels in Wales

- **1401** Henry marries Joan of Navarre

- **1402** Henry enters Wales in pursuit of Glendower

- **1403** Revolt by the Percies: Henry kills Henry Percy (Hotspur) at Shrewsbury

- **1404** Glendower controls Wales, takes title Prince of Wales

- **1406** Prince James of Scotland captured by English on way to France. Robert III of Scotland dies; succeeded by captive James I (to 1420)

- **1409** Glendower's rebellion collapses

- **1410** St Andrew's University, Scotland, founded

- **1411** Henry, Prince of Wales, tries to control government. He is dismissed by Henry IV

Left: **A 15th-century farmhouse. Yeomen or free farmers became increasingly prosperous in this period particularly if they had large flocks of sheep. Farmhouses like this one are still lived in today.**

Below: **Owen Glendower led Wales against England from 1400 to 1409. Defeated, but never captured, his final fate is unknown.**

Henry IV was already troubled by uprisings in England, and Glendower had considerable success. For some years he virtually ruled Wales. But a successful campaign led by Henry's son, the future Henry V, broke the rebellion by 1409. Glendower's territory and castles were taken from him, but he evaded capture and disappeared.

THE CAPTIVE KING OF SCOTLAND

The Stewarts were in many ways an unlucky family. Most of the Stewart rulers came to the throne young, so the country was ruled by nobles in their name. Five of them died violent deaths.

Yet it was a Stewart, James VI of Scotland, who would unite the thrones of England and Scotland as James I of England in 1603, and the Stewarts (spelled Stuarts from then on) reigned until 1714. Queen Elizabeth II is herself descended from a daughter of James I of England (and James VI of Scotland).

The last years of the reign of Robert III of Scotland, in the early 1400s, were dominated by his brother the Duke of Albany, who was governor of the land. He was suspected of murdering Robert's heir, David. To safeguard his second son, James, Robert sent him to France by sea in 1406. English sailors captured the ship and James, who was 10 years old, was taken to London, where he remained a captive for 18 years, until 1424.

Robert went into deep mourning at the news of his son's capture, and died soon afterwards. The prisoner James was proclaimed King of Scotland. In captivity James wrote a long allegorical poem called *The Kingis Quair* (The King's Book). He also became a musician and an athlete.

FOCUS ON PILGRIMS

People of Christian faith in the Middle Ages went on pilgrimages for different reasons. Many went to seek forgiveness for their sins, or as a result of promises they made to God in return for His help. Others went seeking a miracle cure for an illness (just as people still go today to visit Lourdes in France). They visited famous shrines, monasteries and cathedrals around Britain, such as Becket's tomb at Canterbury. But many also travelled overseas, as far away as Jerusalem in the Holy Land.

The medieval pilgrim began his journey with a blessing by a priest, and on his return trip he would wear on his hat the badge of the shrine visited. The ones shown here are from Canterbury Cathedral. Along the way he would find hospices set up specially for pilgrims. Peasants, nuns, knights and merchants journeyed together. Pilgrimages were one of the few reasons many people had in the Middle Ages to travel long distances at home or overseas.

Henry V

DURING THE FINAL YEARS of Henry IV's reign much of the government passed to his son Henry, though the ailing king resisted any suggestion that he should abdicate. When Henry V came to the throne in 1413, he began by declaring a general pardon for his enemies and revived Edward III's old claim to the throne of France, which was occupied by Charles VI, who had suffered from fits of madness for the past 20 years.

The Dukes of Burgundy and Orleans were rivals for power in France. Henry allied himself with the Burgundians. The prospect of a war in France did much to unite the warring factions in England. Henry said to his father: "By your sword you won your crown, and by my sword I will keep it."

HENRY'S FRENCH CAMPAIGN

Henry's military campaign in France began by capturing the town of Harfleur at the mouth of the River Seine. From there he set out with about 5,000 men, 4,000 of them archers, to march east to Calais. The English found their way barred by a French army more than three times as strong. Attempts to negotiate a clear road to safety failed, and Henry resolved on battle. The French unwisely chose a narrow front between two woods, giving them no room to manoeuvre.

THE BATTLE OF AGINCOURT

Once again, against huge odds the English longbow won the day. This was the battle of Agincourt, fought on October 25, 1415; it was over in three hours, with the loss of almost 10,000 French dead and 2,000 captured, and only a few hundred English killed or wounded. Henry returned to England a hero. He had led the battle from the front, wearing his jewelled crown over his helmet. But Henry's army was too weak to attempt taking the French capital, Paris.

Right: **The battle of Agincourt, 1415. A small English army defeated a much larger French one. The English strength was its archers, whose longbows showered the enemy with arrows. The wet weather also bogged the heavily armoured French knights in the mud.**

Right: **Henry V (1413-1422) is chiefly remembered for his victories against the French, including the battle of Agincourt in 1415. He was a chivalrous soldier and sensible ruler, but his gains in France were lost on his death.**

DEATH OF HENRY V

Henry led a much larger expedition to France in 1417. Within three years he was master of Normandy. His ally, the Duke of Burgundy, was murdered by supporters of Charles VI's heir, the dauphin. This united the dauphin's opponents, who supported Henry V's claim to the French throne. Following the Treaty of Troyes in 1420, Henry was accepted as Regent of France, and as King Charles's heir. To cement the agreement Henry married the French King's daughter, Catherine of Valois. But two years later while on another campaign, Henry died of dysentery, a common disease among armies at that time.

Below: **It might take up to an hour for a knight to be fully dressed for battle. His esquire, or attendant, would strap or lace the leg armour on to the belt first, then came the breastplate and backplate and finally the gauntlets and the helmet.**

Left: **Full suit of plate armour**

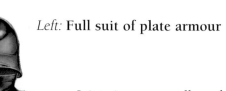

Helmet

Joints in armour allowed some limb movement

Breastplate

A suit of plate armour could weigh 20 to 25 kg

Flexible chain mail underneath

Gauntlet

- **1413** Henry V becomes King of England (to 1422)

- **1415** Invasion of France: Henry captures Harfleur. Battle of Agincourt. Henry founds last monastery before Reformation at Twickenham

- **1417** Henry invades Normandy

- **1420** Treaty of Troyes: Henry to be Regent of France during life of Charles VI, and succeed him. Henry V marries Charles's daughter Catherine. Scottish Regent Albany dies; succeeded by son Murdoch (to 1425)

- **1422** Henry V dies suddenly; succeeded by infant son Henry VI (to 1461). Henry VI's uncles become regents: Humphrey of Gloucester in England; John of Bedford in France

- **1424** James I of Scotland is released, marries Joan Beaufort, and is crowned in Scotland

- **1428** James I calls for election of representatives of sheriffdoms to Scottish Parliament. English lay siege to Orleans in France; Joan of Arc hears "voices"

- **1429** Joan of Arc leads French to relieve city of Orleans. English defeated at Patay. Charles VII crowned King of France at Rheims

- **1430** Burgundian troops take Joan of Arc; hand her over to the English. Statute states shire-knights eligible for Parliament

Above: **A French archer loading a crossbow. The crossbow with its bolt, bowstring and stirrup (*see below right*) was powerful but much slower to load than the English longbow. English archers could fire 10 arrows a minute and their steel-tipped arrows could pierce armoured knights.**

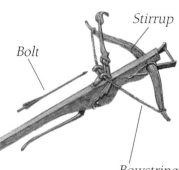

Stirrup

Bolt

Bowstring

Above: **Henry VI (1422-1461) went mad and had to submit his kingdom to a protector, Richard, Duke of York, from 1461 to 1470. He briefly claimed the throne again but was murdered in 1471.**

- **1431** Humphrey of Gloucester crushes Lollard uprising in Abingdon. Henry VI crowned King of France. Joan of Arc burned as a heretic in France

- **1433** Tattershall Castle, Lincolnshire, built with a million bricks

- **1436** Scots defeat English near Berwick

- **1437** Richard, Duke of York, captures Pontoise; Earl of Warwick becomes Regent of France. Murder of James I of Scotland: succeeded by son, James II, aged six (to 1460): Earl of Douglas is regent. Henry VI declared of age, but the Council of State holds power

- **1438** Truce between England and Scotland

- **1439** Congress of Calais: fruitless bid for Anglo-French peace. Henry Beaufort, great-uncle of Henry VI, controls the government. Regent Douglas dies. England makes truce with Burgundy

- *c.* **1440** Johannes Gutenberg invents printing from movable type

HENRY VI

Henry V left his English throne to his baby son, Henry, who was nine months old. Two months after becoming king of England, the baby Henry VI was proclaimed King of France on the death of his mad grandfather, Charles VI. His uncle, Humphrey Duke of Gloucester, was made regent in England. Another uncle, Duke John of Bedford, a skilled and experienced general, ruled France on his behalf. The French claimant to the throne, the dauphin Charles, controlled the country south of the River Loire, but England's hold on the northern region seemed secure.

JOAN OF ARC

In 1428 the demoralized French forces were given unexpected inspiration. Joan of Arc, a young peasant girl from Domrémy on the eastern border of France, heard voices and saw visions which commanded her to free her country from the English. One of the voices was that of the Archangel Michael, who appeared to her in a flood of light and told her to go to the help of the king. Joan went to the dauphin and said: "Gentle dauphin, I am sent to tell you that you shall be anointed and crowned in the town of Rheims, and you shall be lieutenant of the heavenly king who is the King of France".

During the siege of Orleans, Joan of Arc walked unseen through English lines one night during a storm and raised her banner from the battlements of the city to rally the French troops. Under her command the dauphin, Charles, marched to Rheims, where he was crowned King of France. Joan's voices then became silent, and she planned to return home. But she was captured by the Burgundian forces, who were still allied to England, and handed over to the English.

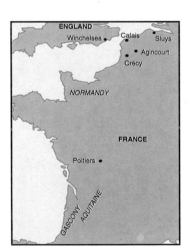

Above: **Map of France showing the main battles of the Hundred Years War, 1337–1453.**

Above: **Joan of Arc (1412-1431) was aged only 17 when she led the French to victory against the English at Orleans.**

Above: **Joan of Arc was tried and found guilty of heresy and sorcery by the Inquisition in 1431. She was burned at the stake by the English in the market place in the French city of Rouen.**

Left: **This was a period of great splendour in clothes for the rich. For men and women in the 1400s, an upper garment with long flowing lines was the most important piece of clothing: for men it could reach the knee, ankle or calf; for women it had long wide sleeves. Both men and women wore long hose, or stockings. For men these could be worn with leather soles attached, or with shoes or boots. Shoes had very long points. Turban-style hats were popular for men. Women favoured elaborate headwear.**

THE HUNDRED YEARS WAR ENDS

Joan of Arc was sold to the English who tried her for witchcraft and heresy, and burned her at the stake. An English soldier saw her die and said: "We are lost; we have burned a saint." In 1435 the valiant Duke of Bedford died, and in the same year the Burgundians finally broke their alliance with the English, and made a treaty with France.

Charles reorganized his army, learning from Joan's inspired victories that the once invincible English archers could be defeated by surprise attacks. Improved French artillery then pounded to ruins English fortresses. By 1453 the English had been almost completely driven out of France, and Henry VI had lost all his father's military conquests. The Hundred Years War was over.

HENRY VI: THE SCHOLAR KING

Henry VI's years as a child king saw bitter conflict between leading nobles competing for influence. When he came of age the situation had not improved; he was a gentle, pious and scholarly man, dominated by the powerful men around him.

When the Duke of Suffolk arranged Henry's marriage to the forceful French princess Margaret of Anjou, he signed a secret treaty ceding Maine to France. The English were furious when they found out. When the Hundred Years War ended in defeat for England, it was said that the Lancastrians, who had seized the throne by force, were unlucky for the country.

THE STRONG MAN OF SCOTLAND

James I of Scotland was released by the regents of Henry VI in 1424, after 18 years in captivity. He took back to Scotland an English bride, Joan Beaufort, granddaughter of John of Gaunt. But he found the land had been badly governed by his cousin Murdoch, son of the late regent, Albany. Within a year he had Murdoch and his sons executed. Within four years James had reorganized the Scottish government, strengthened Parliament, reformed the law courts and curbed the more rebellious of the Highland chiefs. Three of these chiefs he hanged; the rest he released after a short time in prison.

The Printing Revolution

THE CHINESE INVENTED a printing process using wooden blocks in the 6th century AD, and also produced a form of paper to print on. But printing by machines did not appear in Europe until the 1450s. By that time German-born Johannes Gutenberg had invented a printing press with separate pieces of metal type that could be moved around and could print individual letters. This printing method was slow, but the quality was the same for each copy and much easier to read than handwriting. For the first time many copies of a book could be made easily.

CAXTON AND THE FIRST BOOKS

The first book printed in English was produced in the 1470s by William Caxton. Before this, books were copied by hand in universities and monasteries, making them precious and rare. Only priests and nobles could afford to buy them.

William Caxton was born around 1422 in Kent, but moved to Bruges, in what is now Belgium, where for 30 years he was a rich merchant. At the age of 50 he moved to Cologne, in Germany, to learn the printing techniques of that country. In Bruges he set up his first press around 1474. There he produced the first book ever printed in English, a history of the legendary city of Troy, which he had translated himself.

In 1476 Caxton returned to England, encouraged by King Edward IV, and set up the first English press at Westminster, near London. With support from Richard III and Henry VII, Caxton later produced nearly 100 books, including Chaucer's *The Canterbury Tales* (in 1478). Many were printed in English rather than in the usual Latin and French, and some were his own translations of foreign books.

Above: **A page from a book called *Legenda aurea*, printed by William Caxton at his press in Westminster. The picture is a woodcut of St Jerome. Before the first printing presses, there were only about 30,000 to 40,000 books in Britain. By the time of Caxton's death in 1491 there were over nine million.**

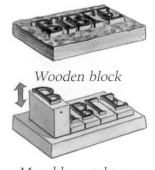

Wooden block

Movable metal type

Above: **Block printing required a carver to cut the letters in reverse in one solid piece of wood, which could be used for only one job. Gutenberg introduced metal type which could be broken up and reused.**

Below: **In the Middle Ages books were not made of paper but of dried animal skins, on which scribes copied out text. The sheets were then stitched together by hand and bound between leather-covered boards.**

In Caxton's time there were often several different English words for one thing and many dialects, or regional variations, of English were spoken. Caxton chose one dialect for his books, and so helped establish a common language throughout the country. Caxton's type of printing press was used for 350 years, until the power-driven press.

HENRY VI AND PLANTAGENET FEUDS

While Henry VI was still a boy, the security of his throne came under threat from feuding uncles and cousins. Chief among them were the Beauforts, the descendants of John of Gaunt and his mistress, Katherine Swynford. The second Beaufort son, Henry, became Bishop of Winchester and was the richest man in the kingdom. Henry Beaufort competed for power with Humphrey, Duke of Gloucester, during Henry VI's minority, and influenced the feeble King when he came of age. These rivalries were to break out into what became known as the Wars of the Roses.

Above: **A printing press. The press was screwed down by hand and this squeezed the paper and type together. The invention of movable metal type meant that books could be produced more quickly and efficiently. Printing was introduced into England by William Caxton in 1476. It helped to spread and establish a common English language instead of local dialects.**

Left: **At first printing was carried out by rubbing an inked woodblock onto a sheet of paper. But Gutenberg invented movable metal type and adapted a wine press to apply pressure evenly over a whole sheet of paper. The ink was spread on a metal plate and then dabbed on the type with a leather-covered tool.**

27

Wars of the Roses

THE WARS OF THE ROSES were a series of conflicts for the English throne between families within the Plantagenet line. The main rivals were the House of York and the House of Lancaster, and these warring houses each had an emblem – the red rose of Lancaster, and the white rose of York – which gave its name to these wars.

The conflict between Lancaster and York was made worse by the barons, who were no longer fighting in France. Henry Beaufort's nephew John, Duke of Somerset, was the commander of Henry V's forces in France. After John's death, his brother Edmund, who became Duke of Somerset, led the English forces in the last battles of the Hundred Years War, and was a possible heir to the throne. Edmund's sister, Joan, married James I of Scotland. Several of the Beauforts died without children and others were killed in the Wars of the Roses.

Above: **The Wars of the Roses get their name from the badges of the two families involved: the red rose of Lancaster and the white rose of York. When Henry VII married Elizabeth of York he combined the two to form the Tudor rose (shown here).**

Right: **A map of England showing the movements and battles of the Yorkist and Lancastrian forces during the Wars of the Roses. The rivalry between the two great families ended with victory for Henry Tudor who was a Lancastrian.**

Below: **The crown of Edward IV, who became undisputed king during the Wars of the Roses after the battle of Tewkesbury in 1471.**

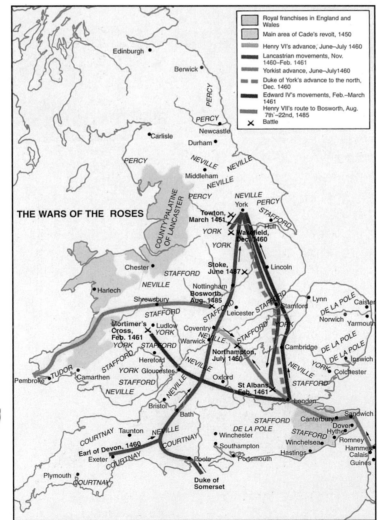

THE WARS OF THE ROSES

Royal franchises in England and Wales
Main area of Cade's revolt, 1450
Henry VI's advance, June–July 1460
Lancastrian movements, Nov. 1460–Feb. 1461
Yorkist advance, June–July 1460
Duke of York's advance to the north, Dec. 1460
Edward IV's movements, Feb.–March 1461
Henry VII's route to Bosworth, Aug. 7th–22nd, 1485
X Battle

- **1440** English recapture Harfleur from the French. Douglas's sons murdered by order of councillors after dining with James II of Scotland

- **1441** Henry VI founds King's College, Cambridge

- **1444** William de la Pole, Duke of Suffolk, negotiates truce with France

- **1445** Henry VI marries Margaret of Anjou

- **1447** Parliament called at Bury St Edmunds, Suffolk. Humphrey of Gloucester arrested and dies in captivity

- **1449** English sack Fougères, Brittany: war with France resumes. Richard of York becomes Lord Lieutenant of Ireland; Edmund, Duke of Somerset, leads English in France

- **1450** Duke of Suffolk accused of selling the realm to France, and is murdered on way to exile. Jack Cade's Rebellion: 30,000 rebels from Kent and Sussex control London for a few days

- **1451** French capture Bordeaux and Bayonne, leaving England only Calais

- **1453** Henry VI becomes insane: York is regent

- **1454** Henry recovers; infant son Edward becomes Prince of Wales

- **1455** Wars of the Roses begin. Battle of St Albans: Yorkist victory. Henry VI captured. York becomes Lord Protector

- **1456** Queen Margaret dismisses York

- **1459** Civil war renewed: Lancastrian victory at battles of Bloreheath and Ludford

- **1460** Battle of Northampton: Yorkists capture Henry VI again. He agrees to York's succession

Above: **The Lancastrian King Henry VI at his Court as shown in an illuminated manuscript. In 1453 Henry suffered the first of several periods** of insanity. **Richard, Duke of York became Protector because Henry was unable to carry out his duties as King of England.**

This left John's daughter, Margaret Beaufort, as the Lancastrian heir. She married Edmund Tudor, Earl of Richmond and was the mother of the future king, Henry VII.

YORK VERSUS LANCASTER

For some years after he married, Henry VI had no heir. There were two obvious candidates for the succession. Richard, Duke of York, was descended through his father from Edward III's youngest son, Edmund, and through his mother from Edward's second son, Lionel. He had a better claim to the throne than the king himself. The other candidate was the Lancastrian Edmund Beaufort, Duke of Somerset. Like Henry VI, Edmund was descended from Edward III's third son, John of Gaunt, but like all Beauforts he was barred from the throne. But he was still a favourite of King Henry and his queen, Margaret of Anjou. York, an honest and competent man, did not press his claim.

FIGHTING BEGINS

In 1453 King Henry went mad. During the same year his wife gave birth to a son, Edward. Law and order had almost completely broken down and unruly groups of soldiers, returned from fighting in France, roamed the countryside. York was made

Lord Protector. Somerset was blamed for defeats in France towards the end of the Hundred Years War, and was sent to the Tower. Almost as suddenly as he went mad, King Henry VI recovered. But Queen Margaret still controlled the king, and she now influenced the dismissal of York as Lord Protector and the release of Somerset.

York still did not openly claim the Crown, but he decided to fight against the hostile Margaret. His army met that of Margaret, Henry and Somerset at St Albans. Somerset was killed, Henry VI was captured and York briefly became Lord Protector again. After a few years of uneasy peace, fighting broke out again and the Lancastrians won. York was killed.

WARWICK THE KINGMAKER

After the death of the Duke of York in 1460, the Yorkist leadership passed to his son, Edward, who was only 19 years old. One of the most powerful nobles, Edward's cousin Richard Neville, Earl of Warwick, became the power behind the throne during the Wars of the Roses. His intrigues gave him the nickname of the Kingmaker. Warwick Castle today provides a spectacular reminder of this turbulent period.

Above: **Warwick Castle, the base for Richard Neville, an important leader in the Wars of the Roses.**

Left: Edward IV (1461-1483) was the first Yorkist king. He was a very tall, handsome and strong leader who brought a period of peace and prosperity to England. During his reign the arts also flourished.

EDWARD OF YORK

In the 1460s the civil war became more intense with each side seeking vengeance for the killing of its own supporters. After several battles, Edward of York entered London and was proclaimed king as Edward IV. Soon afterwards, the battle of Towton crushed the Lancastrians. Despite this, the Lancastrian cause was kept alive by Queen Margaret, who still favoured Edmund Beaufort. Edward IV's marriage to Elizabeth Woodville brought her family to prominence and angered Warwick, who had hoped to arrange a French marriage for the king.

In 1469, Warwick rebelled and captured Edward. Warwick and Edward were reconciled but only briefly, and then Warwick had to flee to France. There, as a price for French help, he allied with his old enemy Queen Margaret. Warwick returned to England and won massive support; Edward in turn had to flee. Warwick restored King Henry VI to the throne, but his second reign lasted only a few months.

EDWARD'S VICTORY

Edward returned to England with troops from Burgundy. At the battle of Barnet (1471) Warwick was killed. At Tewkesbury, a few weeks later, the Lancastrians were finally crushed and many of the great barons killed. Henry VI's son Prince Edward was killed during the battle by Edward IV and his brothers. Yorkist Edward's battle cry had always been: "Kill the nobles and spare the commons!" Edward IV was then undisputed king. Henry VI was put back in the Tower and died shortly after, probably murdered.

Below: The battle of Bosworth Field in Leicestershire. Henry Tudor, who lived in exile in France, invaded England to claim the Crown by force. On August 22, 1485, Richard III was hacked to death by Henry Tudor's forces. In this picture, Henry kneels as he is crowned with a golden coronet. Legend says that the coronet was found on the battlefield from under a gorse bush.

- **1460** James II of Scotland killed by exploding cannon at Roxburgh: succeeded by James III, aged eight (to 1488). Battle of Wakefield: Lancastrian victory. Richard of York killed

- **1461** Battle of Mortimer's Cross: Richard's son, Edward, Duke of York, defeats Lancastrians. Second battle of St Albans: Margaret rescues Henry VI, defeats Earl of Warwick. York assumes the Crown as Edward IV (to 1483). Battle of Towton: Lancastrians defeated. Henry flees to Scotland

- **1462** Warwick crushes Lancastrians

- **1463** Edward again defeats Lancastrians: Margaret flees to France

- **1464** Edward crushes more Lancastrian rebellions. Yorkists capture Henry. Edward marries Elizabeth Woodville

- **1466** Lord Boyd kidnaps James III and becomes governor of Scotland

EDWARD IV: FIRST YORKIST KING

Edward IV proved the strong and efficient ruler England badly needed. Popular demand called for the reconquest of the lost lands in France. He obtained funds through Parliament to finance an invasion but he also accepted money from the French not to invade, thus giving him two sources of income. He pursued a peaceful foreign policy which encouraged trade and kept taxes low. Also a ruthless king, Edward called another Parliament to condemn his treacherous brother George, Duke of Clarence, who died in the Tower.

EDWARD V: THE PRINCE IN THE TOWER

Edward IV had two young sons, and his rule and succession seemed secure. But at the age of 40 he was taken ill, and died within ten days. His 12-year-old son, Edward, succeeded him in 1483. Under the protectorship of his uncle, Richard, Duke of Gloucester, the reign of this young boy lasted just eleven weeks and one day.

Above: **Richard III (1483-1485) was the last Yorkist king. He was an energetic and competent king but made many enemies.**

- **1467** Scottish Parliament bans "fute-ball and golfe"

- **1469** Warwick changes sides, captures Edward IV, but lets him go

- **1470** Warwick forced to flee to France: he and Queen Margaret unite. Warwick lands with an army, restores Henry VI to the throne. Edward flees to Flanders

- **1471** Edward lands in Yorkshire with Flemish troops: resumes Crown. Battle of Barnet: Warwick killed. Battle of Tewkesbury: Prince of Wales killed. Margaret captured and Henry VI murdered in the Tower

- **1473** Edward sets up Council of the Marches to keep order in Wales

- **1475** William Caxton prints first book in English at Bruges. Edward plans to invade France, but is bought off by Louis XI

- **1476** Caxton prints first book in England at his press in Westminster. James III of Scotland subdues rebellion by John, Lord of the Isles

- **1483** Edward dies; succeeded by son Edward V, aged 12. Richard, Duke of Gloucester, is Regent: he declares Edward illegitimate and takes the throne as Richard III (to 1485). Edward and his younger brother disappear

- **1484** Heralds' College is founded. Richard III makes peace with Scots

- **1485** Henry Tudor, Earl of Richmond, invades England. Battle of Bosworth: Richard is killed and Wars of the Roses end. Henry Tudor takes throne as Henry VII

Right: **A famous painting by Sir John Millais in the late 19th century. It shows the two young princes, 12-year-old Edward V and his 9-year-old brother Richard, who were sent to the Tower of London by their uncle Richard III and never seen again. Richard III was so loathed by his enemies that after his death at the battle of Bosworth, he was buried without ceremony and later his bones were thrown out and his coffin used as a horse trough.**

RICHARD III

Richard, Duke of Gloucester, was renowned for his generalship, his abilities as an administrator, and his loyalty to the late king, Edward IV. Richard's strength was in the north but he was hated in the south. The Woodvilles, relatives of Edward's queen, Elizabeth, and Lord Hastings, one of Edward IV's generals, opposed his claim to the throne.

On Edward IV's death in 1483, Richard acted quickly: he accused Hastings of treason, and had him executed within the hour. Richard took Edward V and his young brother to the Tower "for safety"; they were never seen again. He told Parliament that Edward IV's marriage to Elizabeth Woodville (who also disputed Richard's claim) was invalid because Edward had previously made a marriage contract with someone else; the little princes were thus illegitimate. As a result, within three months of Edward IV's death, Parliament asked Richard to accept the Crown. At first Richard appeared to hesitate, but after some persuasion he accepted after all.

The playwright William Shakespeare was later to portray the king as an evil hunchback in his play *Richard III.* But today many historians question whether he was so evil. In 1485 Henry Tudor, the last Lancastrian claimant to the throne, crossed from France and landed at Milford Haven in west Wales. He met Richard at the battle of Bosworth. Richard was deserted by many of his followers and killed. Henry Tudor was generally welcomed as Richard's successor and became Henry VII. The following year he married Edward IV's daughter, Elizabeth of York, thus ending the Wars of the Roses.

RULERS OF BRITAIN

HOUSE	NAME	REIGN	MARRIED	CHILDREN
PLANTAGENET	Henry II	1154 – 1189	Eleanor of Aquitaine	Henry the Young King, Richard I, Geoffrey, John
	Richard I the Lionheart	1189 – 1199	Berengaria of Navarre	
	John	1199 –1216	1. Hadwisa of Gloucester	
			2. Isabella of Angoulême	Henry III, Eleanor (married Simon de Montfort)
	Henry III	1216 – 1272	Eleanor of Provence	Edward I, Margaret (married Alexander III of Scotland), Edmund Crouchback
	Edward I the Lawgiver	1272 – 1307	1. Eleanor of Castile	Edward II
			2. Margaret of France	
	Edward II	1307 – 1327	Isabella of France	Edward III
	Edward III	1327 – 1377	Philippa of Hainault	Edward the Black Prince, Lionel, John of Gaunt, Edmund Duke of York
LANCASTER	Richard II (son of the Black Prince)	1377 – 1399	1. Anne of Bohemia	
			2. Isabella of France	
	Henry IV (son of John of Gaunt)	1399 – 1413	1. Mary de Bohun	Henry V, John Duke of Bedford, Humphrey Duke of Gloucester
			2. Joan of Navarre	
	Henry V	1413 – 1422	Catherine of Valois	Henry VI
	Henry VI	1422 – 1461	Margaret of Anjou	Edward
YORK	Edward IV (descended from Lionel)	1461 – 1483	Elizabeth Woodville	Edward V and Richard (Princes in the Tower), Elizabeth (married Henry VII)
	Edward V	1483		
	Richard III	1483 – 1485	Anne Neville	

GLOSSARY

canonize to formally declare a person a saint. Used by the Roman Catholic Church

cede to give up land to another person or country

crusades a series of wars fought by Christians against Muslims for control of the Holy Land (part of the Middle East). The First Crusade was in 1096, the last in 1291

dauphin title of the direct heir to the French throne

excommunicate to expel from the Church

feudal system (till 1400s) a system under which people held land in exchange for services to a noble

heresy a religious belief that is against the usual, accepted form of religion

homage a public acknowledgement of respect or honour to a lord or superior

Inquisition a search or enquiry by the Roman Catholic Church into heresy, sometimes involving the torture and execution of disbelievers

Justiciar chief officer of state, Lord Chief Justice

mandate a command from a superior, such as the Pope, ordering a person how to act

medieval of the Middle Ages

Muslims followers of Islam; those who worship Allah and follow the teachings of Mohammed

Parliament Britain's highest governing body, which had its beginnings in the Middle Ages

pilgrimage a journey to a sacred shrine at home or abroad to give thanks or seek religious salvation

Plantagenet originally the nickname of Geoffrey of Anjou from the sprig of broom, *planta genista*, which he wore as a badge

regent person who rules while monarch is either too young (known as a minority), too ill or too far abroad to govern effectively at home

Wars of the Roses conflicts between Yorkists and Lancastrians for the English throne, 1455-1485.

INDEX

ACKNOWLEDGMENTS

The publisher would like to thank the following for supplying additional illustrations for this book:

Picture research: Alex Goldberg, Elaine Willis

page 3, medieval market, Mark Peppé; p7, Magna Carta, The Bridgeman Art Library; p18, Henry V, The Bridgeman Art Library; p20, Henry IV, Mark Peppé; p21, pilgrim badges, Mark Peppé; p29, Henry VI, Art Archive/British Library; p29 Warwick Castle, iStock/Lovattpics; p32, Princes in the Tower, The Bridgeman Art Library

Quick & Easy
Simple
Mediterranean

p

Contents

Introduction

Just a brief stay anywhere in the Mediterranean leaves an enduring memory of the wonderful aromas and robust flavours of the food. Intensity of flavour is the one quality that unites the cuisines of southern France, Italy, and Spain with those of Greece, Turkey, and the North African countries. The range of dishes of these coastal regions is as diverse as their peoples. They have evolved from the simple fare produced for generations from abundant local ingredients. All the recipes in this book are easy to prepare, but their very simplicity means that to capture authentic Mediterranean flavours in your cooking you will need to search for authentic ingredients of the high quality and ripeness you would buy in the region's stores and markets.

Olive Oil

All the Mediterranean countries share many ingredients, and olive oil is the principal one. There are numerous varieties, ranging in colour from almost emerald green to palest yellow, with flavours intensifying from mild to peppery to spicy. There are even oils with a hint of chocolate. If you cook with other vegetable oils, such as sunflower or corn oils, olive oil may be an acquired taste. The only way to find the type you like most is to taste many. Some delicatessens specializing in Mediterranean produce offer free tastings.

Olive oils are graded from cooking quality oil which is simply labelled 'Olive Oil' and is the cheapest, to extra-virgin oil, the most expensive. This is produced from the first pressing of the olives and so has the fullest flavour. It should be used in salad dressings and other dishes of uncooked ingredients, since heating the oil diminishes its flavour. For cooked dishes, always use a cooking oil. Olive oil contains very little saturated fat - the type of fat which may be linked to heart disease, but it is a fat and should be used sparingly.

Tomatoes

Sun-ripened tomatoes seem synonymous with the food of the region, flavouring cooked and uncooked dishes. When you can buy only insipid early-ripened tomatoes, a quality canned variety is better for cooked dishes.

Italian plum tomatoes are best for most Mediterranean dishes, but beefsteak tomatoes and the small cherry tomatoes are ideal for many recipes.

Garlic

Garlic is an important flavouring in many Mediterranean dishes. It may be cooked or used raw. When it is cooked slowly, its strong flavour softens and it becomes soft and deliciously sweet. Do not buy garlic bulbs that have sprouted, because they may taste bitter. The best garlic has compact cloves and tight-fitting skin. Do not store garlic in the refrigerator; it keeps best in a dark place at room temperature, which is why many people use garlic pots with small holes for air to circulate.

Aubergines

Egg-shaped aubergines, also called eggplants, with their deep-purple, smooth skins, feature strongly in cooking throughout the Mediterranean. They are an essential ingredient in French and Italian food. Sprinkle cut pieces of aubergine with salt and leave them to stand for about 30 minutes before using. This draws out moisture which prevents the flesh from becoming soggy, and helps eliminate the bitterness which is a characteristic of older aubergines. After they have drained, rinse them well to remove excess salt. If the aubergine slices are to be baked or fried, pat them dry with paper towels.

In summer, Mediterranean market stalls are piled high with miniature aubergine varieties, which may have pale purple or almost-white skins. Local chefs use these to make attractive appetizers or edible garnishes. Buy aubergines only if they feel smooth and firm. Size does not affect the flavour, but the thicker an aubergine is, the more seeds it is likely to contain. Aubergines have a natural affinity with tomatoes, so the two ingredients are combined in many Mediterranean dishes.

Seafood

Fish and shellfish have a major role in the cooking of the Mediterranean. There is one golden rule for purchasing both: buy only the freshest, and cook it on the same day. Fresh fish have clear, shiny eyes and red gills. A fresh whole fish will be firm, not floppy. If it droops, it has been out of the water for more than a day. Cut fillets and steaks of swordfish and tuna should have a clear, clean-looking surface. Sea bass and other white fish should have a pearly colour quality.

Fish should not smell fishy. Instead, it should have the fresh, almost sweet aroma of a fish that was taken from the water only a few hours before you picked it up.

Shellfish, such as mussels, oysters and clams, should still be alive when sold. If they are fresh, their shells will

be closed. Prawns, on the other hand, are usually frozen before they are packed and shipped. As a general rule, the less time taken to cook seafood, the better the flavour and texture will be.

Fresh Herbs

Summer dishes are flavoured with the aromatic herbs which grow in the Mediterranean region. Winter stews and casseroles are enhanced with dried herbs. Only fresh herbs contribute their full flavour, so buy cut or growing herbs rather than dried ones. Buy vibrant-looking herbs, because limp herbs without their full aroma will add little to a dish. Greenhouse herbs can lack flavour, so sniff them before buying. Alternatively, grow your own.

Basil This fragrant herb is frequently used in pasta dishes and soups. It marries perfectly with tomatoes. It is hard to preserve, since the leaves turn black if frozen, and lose their aroma. If you have a glut, layer leaves with sea salt in a non-metal container, cover it tightly, and leave for 3 months. The dried basil can be added to cooked dishes. Alternatively, freeze large quantities of Pesto Sauce (see page 21).

Coriander This is a herb often called for in Moroccan, Turkish and Greek recipes, but is more familiar to many people as an ingredient of Asian cooking. It looks rather like to flat-leaved parsley and the most reliable way to tell them apart is to taste a leaf. Use coriander in soups, with seafood recipes, and with pickles.

Dill This feathery green herb with its distinctive flavour goes well with all seafood and tomato dishes, and is particularly used in Greek cooking.

Parsley Mediterranean cooks favour the flat-leaved variety of this all-purpose herb. Always buy it fresh or frozen, never dried. Use it in salads and as a garnish.

Marjoram The Greeks call this herb the 'joy of the mountains' and it is prominent in the islands' cuisines. It is best with pork and poultry dishes.

Oregano This herb is also called wild marjoram. It is pungent and should be used sparingly. However, it dries well, retaining its flavour. It is traditionally added to winter casseroles and pizza toppings, but also try it with tomato, courgette, and aubergine dishes.

Rosemary This is a strongly flavoured and scented shrub and may be used cooked and uncooked, fresh or dried. It is a natural partner to lamb. If you use it uncooked, choose only young shoots.

Sage Fresh and dried sage are popular in Italian cooking. Sage has a strong flavour and should be used sparingly. Boil it with beans and use it to flavour grilled poultry.

Thyme Use the aromatic leaves to flavour tomatoes, stews and grilled meats, and to accompany olives.

KEY	
🐚	Simplicity level 1 – 3 (1 easiest, 3 slightly harder)
🍲	Preparation time
🕐	Cooking time

Provençal Fish Soup

For the best results, you need to use flavourful fish, such as cod or haddock. Frozen fish fillets are suitable.

NUTRITIONAL INFORMATION

Calories 122   Sugars 6g
Protein .... 12g   Fat 3g
Carbohydrate ... 7g   Saturates 0.1g

🐻 🐻

🍲 1 hr 10 mins   🕐 10 mins

SERVES 4–6

INGREDIENTS

1 tbsp olive oil

2 onions, finely chopped

1 small leek, thinly sliced

1 small carrot, finely chopped

1 celery stick, finely chopped

1 small fennel bulb, finely chopped (optional)

3 garlic cloves, finely chopped

225 ml/8 fl oz dry white wine

400 g/14 oz canned tomatoes in juice

1 bay leaf

pinch of fennel seeds

2 strips orange rind

¼ tsp saffron threads

1.2 litres/2 pints water

350 g/12 oz skinless white fish fillets

salt and pepper

garlic croûtons, to serve

1 Heat the oil in a large saucepan over a medium heat. Add the onions and cook for about 5 minutes, stirring frequently, until softened. Add the leek, carrot, celery, fennel and garlic and continue cooking for 4–5 minutes, or until the leek is wilted.

2 Add the wine and let it bubble for a minute. Add the tomatoes, bay leaf, fennel seeds, orange rind, saffron and water. Bring just to the boil, reduce the heat, cover and cook gently, stirring occasionally, for 30 minutes.

3 Add the fish and cook for a further 20–30 minutes, or until it is very soft and flaky. Remove the bay leaf and orange rind if possible.

4 Allow the soup to cool slightly, then transfer to a blender or food processor and purée until smooth, working in batches if necessary. (If using a food processor, strain off the cooking liquid and reserve. Purée the soup solids with enough cooking liquid to moisten them, then combine with the remaining liquid.)

5 Return the soup to the saucepan. Taste and adjust the seasoning, if necessary, and simmer for 5–10 minutes, or until heated through. Ladle the soup into warm bowls and sprinkle with croûtons.

Greek Bean Soup

This is based on a simple and variable bean soup typical of Greek home cooking. The artichoke hearts make it a bit fancier and more interesting.

NUTRITIONAL INFORMATION

Calories 109   Sugars 7g
Protein .... 6g   Fat 3g
Carbohydrate .. 16g   Saturates 0.1g

15 mins   40 mins

SERVES 6

INGREDIENTS

1 tbsp olive oil

1 large onion, finely chopped

1 large carrot, finely diced

2 celery sticks, finely chopped

4 tomatoes, skinned, deseeded and chopped, or 250 g/9 oz drained canned tomatoes

2 garlic cloves, finely chopped

800 g/28 oz canned cannellini or haricot beans, drained and rinsed well

1.2 litres/2 pints water

1 courgette, finely diced

grated rind of ½ lemon

1 tbsp chopped fresh mint, or ¼ tsp dried mint

1 tsp chopped fresh thyme, or ⅛ tsp dried thyme

1 bay leaf

400 g/14 oz canned artichoke hearts

2 Add the beans and water. Bring to the boil, reduce the heat, cover and cook gently for about 10 minutes.

3 Add the courgette, lemon rind, mint, thyme and bay leaf and season with salt and pepper. Cover and simmer about 40 minutes, or until all the vegetables are tender. Allow to cool slightly. Transfer 450 ml/16 fl oz to a blender or a food processor, purée until smooth, and recombine.

4 Meanwhile, heat the remaining oil in a frying pan over a medium heat, adding more if necessary to coat the bottom of the pan. Fry the artichokes, cut side down, until lightly browned. Turn over and fry long enough to heat through.

5 Ladle the soup into warm bowls and top each with an artichoke heart.

1 Heat 1 teaspoon of the olive oil in a large saucepan over a medium heat. Add the onion and cook for 3–4 minutes, stirring occasionally, until the onion softens. Add the carrot, celery, tomatoes and garlic and continue cooking for another 5 minutes, stirring frequently.

Hummus & Courgette Soup

This light and elegant soup could not be easier. Its subtle flavour makes it a great starter, especially when entertaining vegetarians.

NUTRITIONAL INFORMATION

Calories ...... 135 Sugars 3g
Protein .... 5g Fat 9g
Carbohydrate ... 8g Saturates 0.1g

🐚 🐚

🍲 5 mins   🕐 25 mins

SERVES 4

I N G R E D I E N T S

1 tsp olive oil

1 small onion

3 courgettes, sliced (about 450 g/1 lb)

450 ml/16 fl oz vegetable or chicken stock

175 g/6 oz ready-made hummus

fresh lemon juice, to taste

salt and pepper

finely chopped fresh parsley, to garnish

1 Heat the oil in a saucepan over a medium heat. Add the onion and courgettes, cover and cook for about 3 minutes, stirring occasionally, until they begin to soften.

2 Add the stock and season lightly with salt and pepper. Bring to the boil, reduce the heat, cover and cook gently for about 20 minutes, or until the vegetables are tender.

3 Allow the soup to cool slightly, then transfer to a blender or food processor and purée until smooth. (If using a food processor, strain off the cooking liquid and reserve. Purée the soup solids with enough cooking liquid to moisten them, then combine with the remaining liquid.)

4 Add the hummus to the puréed soup in the blender or processor and process to combine.

5 Return the soup to the saucepan and reheat gently over a medium-low heat. Taste and adjust the seasoning, adding a little lemon juice if wished. Ladle into warm bowls, sprinkle with parsley and serve.

COOK'S TIP
If you wish, peel the courgettes. It gives the soup a nice pale colour.

Chicken & Mushroom Soup

This soup needs a rich stock, and the mushrooms contribute plenty of extra flavour. The pastry top is baked separately to simplify serving.

NUTRITIONAL INFORMATION

Calories 513   Sugars 2g
Protein .... 28g   Fat 33g
Carbohydrate .. 44g   Saturates 10g

15 mins   50 mins

SERVES 6

I N G R E D I E N T S

1.5 litres/2¾ pints stock

4 skinless boned chicken breasts

2 garlic cloves, crushed

small bunch of fresh tarragon or
¼ tsp dried tarragon

1 tbsp butter

400 g/14 oz chestnut or horse mushrooms,
sliced

3 tbsp dry white wine

6 tbsp plain flour

175 ml/6 fl oz whipping or double cream

375 g/13 oz puff pastry

2 tbsp finely chopped fresh parsley

salt and pepper

1 Put the stock in a saucepan and bring just to the boil. Add the chicken, garlic and tarragon, reduce the heat, cover and simmer for 20 minutes, or until the chicken is cooked through. Remove the chicken and strain the stock. When the chicken is cool, cut into bite-sized pieces.

2 Melt the butter in a large frying pan over a medium heat. Add the mushrooms and season with salt and pepper. Cook for 5–8 minutes, or until they are golden brown, stirring occasionally at first, then stirring more often after they start to colour. Add the wine and bubble briefly. Remove the mushrooms from the heat.

3 Put the flour in a small mixing bowl and very slowly whisk in the cream to make a thick paste. Stir in a little of the stock to make a smooth liquid.

4 Bring the strained stock to the boil in a large saucepan. Whisk in the flour mixture and bring back to the boil. Boil gently for 3–4 minutes, or until the soup thickens, stirring frequently. Add the cooked mushrooms and liquid, if any. Reduce the heat to low and simmer very gently, just to keep warm.

5 Cut out 6 rounds of pastry smaller in diameter than the soup bowls, using a plate as a guide. Put on a baking sheet, prick with a fork and bake in a preheated oven at 200°C/400°F/Gas Mark 6 for about 15 minutes, or until deep golden.

6 Meanwhile, add the chicken to the soup. Taste and adjust the seasoning. Simmer for about 10 minutes, or until the soup is heated through. Stir in the parsley. Ladle the soup into warm bowls and place the pastry rounds on top. Serve immediately.

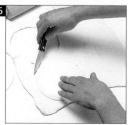

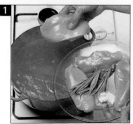

Giant Garlic Prawns

In Spain, giant garlic prawns are cooked in small half-glazed earthenware dishes called *cazuelas*. The prawns arrive sizzling at your table.

NUTRITIONAL INFORMATION

Calories 385	Sugars 0g
Protein 26g	Fat 31g
Carbohydrate ... 1g	Saturates 5g

5 mins   5 mins

SERVES 4

INGREDIENTS

125 ml/4 fl oz olive oil

4 garlic cloves, finely chopped

2 hot red chillies, deseeded and finely chopped

450 g/1 lb cooked king prawns

2 tbsp chopped fresh flat-leaved parsley

salt and pepper

crusty bread, to serve

lemon wedges, to garnish

COOK'S TIP
If you can buy raw prawns, cook them as above, but increase the cooking time to 5–6 minutes, or until the prawns are cooked through and turn bright pink.

1 Heat the oil in a large frying pan over a low heat. Add the garlic and chillies and cook for 1–2 minutes, or until softened but not coloured.

2 Add the prawns and stir-fry for about 2–3 minutes, or until heated through and coated in the oil and garlic mixture. Remove from the heat.

3 Add the parsley and stir well to mix. Season to taste.

4 Divide the prawns and garlicky oil between warmed serving dishes and serve with lots of crusty bread. Garnish with lemon wedges.

Hummus

Quick and easy to make, this dip features regularly on Mediterranean menus. Serve it with fingers of pitta bread or vegetable sticks for dipping.

NUTRITIONAL INFORMATION

Calories 204   Sugars 1g
Protein .... 7g   Fat 14g
Carbohydrate .. 13g   Saturates 2g

12 hrs soaking, plus 10 mins   1¼ hrs

SERVES 4

INGREDIENTS

200 g/7 oz dried chickpeas

2 large garlic cloves

7 tbsp extra-virgin olive oil

2½ tbsp tahini

1 tbsp lemon juice, or to taste

salt and pepper

TO GARNISH

extra-virgin olive oil

paprika

fresh coriander

1 Place the chickpeas in a large bowl. Pour in at least twice the volume of cold water to beans and leave to stand for at least 12 hours, until they double in size.

2 Drain the chickpeas. Put them in a large flameproof casserole or saucepan and add twice the volume of water to beans. Bring to the boil and boil hard for 10 minutes, skimming the surface of the liquid.

3 Lower the heat and simmer for 1 hour, skimming the surface if necessary, until the chickpeas are tender. Cut the garlic cloves in half, discard the pale green or white cores and coarsely chop. Set aside.

4 Drain the chickpeas, reserving about 4 tablespoons of the cooking liquid. Put the olive oil, garlic, tahini and lemon juice in a food processor and blend until a smooth paste forms.

5 Add the chickpeas and pulse until they are finely ground but the hummus is still lightly textured. Add a little of the reserved cooking liquid if the mixture is too thick. Season with salt and pepper to taste.

6 Transfer to a bowl, cover with cling film and chill until ready to serve. To serve, drizzle with some olive oil, sprinkle a little paprika over and garnish with fresh coriander. Serve with pitta bread.

Tapenade

These robust olive and anchovy spreads can be as thick or as thin as you like. They make enticing appetizers spread on toasted bread.

NUTRITIONAL INFORMATION

Calories	 227	Sugars	. . . . 0g
Protein	. . . . 5g	Fat	. . . . 23g
Carbohydrate	. . . 0g	Saturates	. . . . . . 3g

20 mins   0 mins

SERVES 4–6

INGREDIENTS

thin slices of day-old baguette (optional)

olive oil (optional)

finely chopped fresh flat-leaved parsley sprigs, to garnish

BLACK OLIVE TAPENADE

250 g/9 oz black Niçoise olives in brine, rinsed and stoned

1 large garlic clove

2 tbsp walnut pieces

4 canned anchovy fillets, drained

about 125 ml/4 fl oz extra-virgin olive oil

lemon juice, to taste

pepper

GREEN OLIVE TAPENADE

250 g/9 oz green olives in brine, rinsed and stoned

4 canned anchovy fillets, rinsed

4 tbsp blanched almonds

1 tbsp bottled capers in brine or vinegar, rinsed

about 125 ml/4 fl oz extra-virgin olive oil

½–1 tbsp finely grated orange rind

pepper

1 To make the black olive tapenade, put the olives, garlic, walnut pieces and anchovies in a food processor and process until blended.

2 With the motor running, slowly add the olive oil through the feed tube, as if making mayonnaise. Add lemon juice and pepper to taste. Transfer to a bowl, cover with cling film and chill until required.

3 To make the green olive tapenade, put the olives, anchovies, almonds and capers in a food processor and process until blended. With the motor running, slowly add the olive oil through the feed tube, as if making mayonnaise. Add orange rind, and pepper to taste. Transfer to a bowl, cover with cling film and chill until required.

4 To serve on croûtes, toast the slices of bread on both sides until crisp. Brush one side of each slice with a little olive oil while they are still hot, so the oil is absorbed.

5 Spread the croûtes with the tapenade of your choice and garnish with parsley.

Roasted Pepper Soup

Ripe, juicy tomatoes and sweet red peppers are roasted to enhance their delicious flavours in this delicate soup.

NUTRITIONAL INFORMATION

Calories	 54	Sugars	. . . . 9g
Protein	. . . . 2g	Fat	. . . . 1g
Carbohydrate	. . 10g	Saturates	. . . . . . 0g

🗑 🗑 🗑

🥗 15 mins   🕙 55 mins

SERVES 6–8

INGREDIENTS

1 kg/2 lb 4 oz juicy plum tomatoes, halved

2 large red peppers, cored, deseeded and halved

1 onion, quartered

3 sprigs fresh dill, tied together, plus a little extra to garnish

1 thin piece of orange rind

juice of 1 orange

600 ml/1 pint vegetable stock

1–1½ tbsp red wine vinegar

salt and pepper

crusty bread, to serve

1 Place the halved plum tomatoes and peppers on a baking sheet, cut-sides up. Add the onion quarters. Place in an oven preheated to 230°C/450°F/ Gas Mark 8 and roast for 20–25 minutes, or until the vegetables just char on the edges.

2 Transfer to a large flameproof casserole or a stockpot. Add the dill, orange rind and juice, stock and salt and pepper to taste. Bring to the boil.

3 Lower the heat, partially cover and simmer for 25 minutes. Remove the dill, transfer the ingredients to a food mill (see Cook's Tip), and purée, or pass through a food processor and a fine sieve.

4 Return the soup to the rinsed casserole or stockpot and reheat. Stir in the vinegar and season if necessary. Ladle into bowls and garnish with dill. Serve hot with crusty bread.

COOK'S TIP

A food mill, or mouli-legume as it is called in France, is ideal for puréeing vegetable soups and sauces because it removes the skin and seeds in the process.

Parma Ham with Fruit

In this classic Italian starter, the slightly salty flavour of air-cured Parma ham provides a marvellous contrast to the sweet fresh fruit.

NUTRITIONAL INFORMATION

Calories 198	Sugars 13g
Protein 16g	Fat 10g
Carbohydrate .. 13g	Saturates 3g

10 mins   0 mins

SERVES 4

INGREDIENTS

1 cantaloupe or charentais melon

4 ripe fresh figs (optional)

12 wafer-thin slices Parma ham

olive oil, to drizzle

pepper

fresh parsley sprigs, to garnish

1 Cut the melon in half lengthways. Using a spoon, scoop out the seeds and discard them. Cut each half into 8 thin wedges. Using a paring knife, cut the rind off each slice.

2 Cut the stems off the figs, if using, but do not peel them. Stand the figs upright with the pointed end upwards. Cut each into quarters without cutting all the way through, so you can open them out into attractive 'flowers'.

COOK'S TIP

For an attractive presentation, you can also prepare all the ingredients on one large serving platter and let guests help themselves.

3 Arrange 3–4 slices of Parma ham on individual serving plates and top with the melon slices and fig 'flowers', if using. Alternatively, arrange the melon slices on the plates and completely cover with the ham; add the figs, if using.

4 Drizzle with olive oil, then grind a little pepper over the top. Garnish with parsley and serve at once.

Greek Salad

Tomatoes and black olives are a classic Mediterranean combination, but Greek cooks add feta, and also honey to draw out the full tomato flavour.

NUTRITIONAL INFORMATION

Calories 347	Sugars 6g
Protein 12g	Fat 31g
Carbohydrate . . . 6g	Saturates 11g

10 mins · 0 mins

SERVES 4

INGREDIENTS

250 g/9 oz feta cheese

250 g/9 oz cucumber

250 g/9 oz Greek kalamata olives

1 red onion or 4 spring onions

2 large juicy tomatoes

1 tsp honey

4 tbsp extra-virgin olive oil

½ lemon

salt and pepper

fresh or dried oregano, to garnish

pitta bread, to serve

1 Drain the feta cheese if it is packed in brine. Place it on a chopping board and cut into 2 cm/¾ inch dice. Transfer to a salad bowl.

2 Cut the cucumber in half lengthways and use a teaspoon to scoop out the seeds. Cut the flesh into 2 cm/¾ inch slices. Add to the bowl with the feta cheese.

3 Stone the olives with an olive or cherry pitter, slice the red onion or finely chop the spring onions and add .

4 Cut each tomato into quarters and scoop out the seeds. Cut the flesh into bite-sized pieces and add to the bowl.

5 Toss the ingredients using your hands. Stir the honey into the olive oil (see Cook's Tip), add to the salad with lemon juice and seasoning to taste. Cover and chill.

6 Garnish with the oregano and serve with pitta bread.

Lemon Risotto

This is a stylish first course, with an aroma and a fresh taste that stimulates the appetite for the meal to follow.

NUTRITIONAL INFORMATION

Calories	442	Sugars	3g
Protein	6g	Fat	15g
Carbohydrate	68g	Saturates	6g

5 mins · 30 mins

SERVES 4

INGREDIENTS

2–3 lemons

2 tbsp olive oil

2 shallots, finely chopped

300 g/10½ oz risotto rice

125 ml/4 fl oz dry white vermouth

1 litre/1¾ pints vegetable or chicken stock, simmering

1 tbsp very, very finely chopped fresh flat-leaved parsley

2 tbsp butter

freshly pared Parmesan cheese, to serve

TO GARNISH

thin strips of pared lemon rind

fresh parsley sprigs

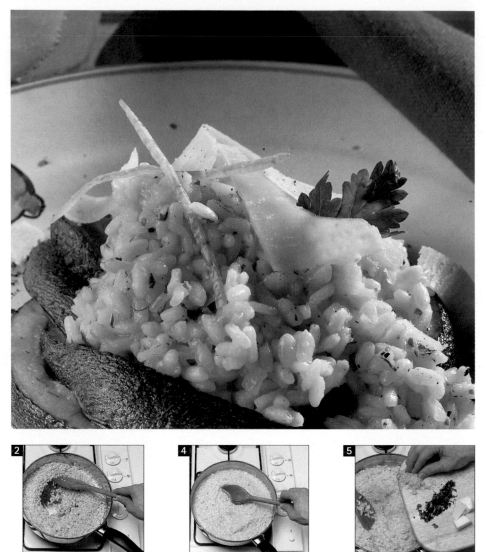

1 Finely grate the rind from 2 lemons. Firmly roll the rindless lemons backwards and forwards on a board, then squeeze 100 ml/3½ fl oz juice. If you don't have enough, squeeze another lemon. Set the rind and juice aside.

2 Heat the olive oil in a heavy-based saucepan. Add the finely chopped shallots and fry, stirring, for about 3 minutes until soft. Add the rice and stir until all the grains are well coated.

3 Stir in the vermouth and bubble until it evaporates. Lower the heat to medium–low. Add the lemon juice and a ladleful of simmering stock. Stir together, then leave to simmer, uncovered, only stirring occasionally, until all the liquid has been absorbed.

4 Add another ladleful of stock and stir, then leave to simmer until absorbed. Continue adding stock in this way, allowing it to be absorbed after each addition, until all the stock has been used and the risotto is creamy, with several tablespoons of liquid floating on the surface.

5 Stir in the lemon rind and parsley. Add the butter, cover, remove from the heat and leave to stand for 5 minutes. Stir well and then garnish with lemon strips and parsley. Serve with Parmesan cheese and avocado slices.

Aïoli

This garlic mayonnaise features in many Provençal recipes, but also makes a delicious dip for a selection of raw and lightly cooked vegetables.

NUTRITIONAL INFORMATION

Calories	239	Sugars	0.1g
Protein	1g	Fat	26g
Carbohydrate	1g	Saturates	4g

5 mins   0 mins

SERVES 4

INGREDIENTS

4 large garlic cloves, or to taste

good pinch of sea salt

2 large egg yolks

300 ml/10 fl oz extra-virgin olive oil

1–2 tbsp lemon juice, to taste

1 tbsp fresh white breadcrumbs

freshly ground black pepper

TO SERVE (OPTIONAL)

a selection of raw vegetables, such as sliced red peppers, courgette slices, whole spring onions and tomato wedges

a selection of blanched and cooled vegetables, such as baby artichoke hearts, cauliflower or broccoli florets or green beans

1 Finely chop the garlic on a chopping board. Sprinkle the salt over the garlic and use the tip and broad side of a knife to work this into a smooth paste.

2 Transfer the garlic paste to a food processor. Add the egg yolks and process until well blended, scraping down the side of the bowl with a rubber spatula, if necessary.

3 With the motor running, slowly pour in the olive oil in a steady steam through the feed tube, processing until a thick mayonnaise forms.

4 Add 1 tablespoon of the lemon juice and the fresh breadcrumbs and quickly process again. Taste and add more lemon juice if necessary. Season to taste with salt and pepper.

5 Place the aïoli in a bowl, cover and chill until ready to serve. This will keep for up to 7 days in the refrigerator. To serve as a dip, place the bowl of aïoli on a large platter and surround with a selection of crudités.

COOK'S TIP

The amount of garlic in a traditional Provençal aïoli is a matter of personal taste. Local cooks use 2 cloves per person as a rule of thumb, but this version is slightly milder, although still bursting with flavour.

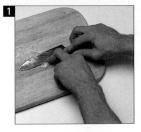

Spinach & Anchovy Pasta

This colourful light meal can be made with a variety of different pasta, including spaghetti and linguine.

NUTRITIONAL INFORMATION

Calories	 619	Sugars	.... 5g
Protein	.... 21g	Fat	.... 31g
Carbohydrate	.. 67g	Saturates	...... 3g

🐾 🐾

🥗 10 mins   🕐 25 mins

SERVES 4

I N G R E D I E N T S

900 g/2 lb fresh, young spinach leaves

400 g/14 oz dried fettuccine

6 tbsp olive oil

3 tbsp pine kernels

3 garlic cloves, crushed

8 canned anchovy fillets, drained and chopped

salt

1 Trim off any tough spinach stalks. Rinse the spinach leaves and place them in a large saucepan with only the water that is clinging to them after washing. Cover and cook over a high heat, shaking the pan from time to time, until the spinach has wilted, but retains its colour. Drain well, set aside and keep warm.

2 Bring a large saucepan of lightly salted water to the boil. Add the fettuccine and 1 tablespoon of the oil and cook for 8–10 minutes, or until it is just tender, but still firm to the bite.

3 Meanwhile, heat 4 tablespoons of the remaining oil in a saucepan. Add the pine kernels and fry until just golden. Remove the pine kernels from the pan and set aside until required.

4 Add the garlic to the pan and fry until golden. Add the anchovies and stir in the wilted spinach. Cook, stirring, for 2–3 minutes, or until heated through. Return the pine kernels to the pan.

5 Drain the fettuccine, toss in the remaining olive oil and transfer to a warm serving dish. Spoon the anchovy and spinach sauce over the fettuccine, toss lightly and serve immediately.

COOK'S TIP

If you are in a hurry, you can use frozen spinach. Thaw and drain it thoroughly, pressing out as much moisture as possible. Cut the leaves into strips and add to the dish with the anchovies in step 4.

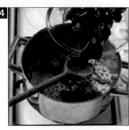

Tuscan Bean Soup

This thick, satisfying blend of beans and diced vegetables in a rich red wine and tomato stock makes an ideal simple supper.

NUTRITIONAL INFORMATION

Calories 160	Sugars 10g
Protein 9g	Fat 2g
Carbohydrate .. 23g	Saturates 0g

10 mins · 25 mins

SERVES 4

I N G R E D I E N T S

1 medium onion, chopped

1 garlic clove, finely chopped

2 celery sticks, sliced

1 large carrot, diced

400 g/14 oz canned chopped tomatoes

150 ml/5 fl oz Italian dry red wine

1.2 litres/2 pints fresh vegetable stock

1 tsp dried oregano

425 g/15 oz canned mixed beans and pulses

2 medium courgettes, diced

1 tbsp tomato purée

salt and pepper

TO SERVE

pesto (see page 21)

crusty bread

1 Place the prepared onion, garlic, celery and carrot in a large saucepan. Stir in the tomatoes, red wine, vegetable stock and oregano.

2 Bring the vegetable mixture to the boil, cover and leave to simmer for 15 minutes. Stir the beans and courgettes into the mixture, and continue to cook, uncovered, for a further 5 minutes.

3 Add the tomato purée to the mixture and season well with salt and pepper to taste. Then heat through, stirring occasionally, for a further 2–3 minutes, but do not allow the mixture to boil again.

4 Ladle the soup into warm bowls and serve with a spoonful of pesto on each portion and accompanied with crusty bread.

VARIATION

For a more substantial soup, add 350 g/12 oz diced lean cooked chicken or turkey with the beans and courgettes in step 2.

Capri Salad

This tomato, olive and Mozzarella salad, dressed with balsamic vinegar and olive oil, makes a delicious starter on its own.

NUTRITIONAL INFORMATION

Calories	 95	Sugars 3g
Protein	.... 3g	Fat 8g
Carbohydrate	... 3g	Saturates 3g

10 mins   0 mins

SERVES 4

INGREDIENTS

2 beef tomatoes

125 g/4½ oz mozzarella cheese

12 black olives

8 basil leaves

1 tbsp balsamic vinegar

1 tbsp olive oil

salt and pepper

basil leaves, to garnish

1 Using a sharp knife, cut the tomatoes into thin slices.

2 Using a sharp knife, cut the mozzarella into slices.

3 Remove the stone from the olives and slice them thinly into rings.

COOK'S TIP

Buffalo mozzarella cheese, although it is usually more expensive because of the comparative rarety of buffalo, does have a better flavour than the cow's milk variety. It is popular in salads, but also provides a tangy layer in baked dishes.

4 Layer the tomato, mozzarella cheese olives and basil in a stack, finishing with a layer of cheese on top.

5 Place each stack under a preheated hot grill for 2–3 minutes, or just long enough to melt the mozzarella.

6 Drizzle over the vinegar and olive oil, and season to taste with a little salt and pepper.

7 Transfer each stack to individual serving plates and garnish with basil leaves. Serve immediately.

Sardines with Pesto

This tasty supper dish works well with small oily fish such as herrings and pilchards, as well as sardines. Use a quality ready-made pesto for speed.

NUTRITIONAL INFORMATION

Calories	 617	Sugars	.... 0.1g
Protein	.... 27g	Fat	.... 56g
Carbohydrate	... 1g	Saturates	..... 11g

20 mins   6 mins

SERVES 4

INGREDIENTS

16 large sardines, scaled and gutted

lemon wedges, to serve

PESTO

50 g/1¾ oz fresh basil leaves

2 garlic cloves, crushed

2 tbsp pine kernels, toasted

50 g/1¾ oz freshly grated Parmesan cheese

150 ml/5 fl oz olive oil

salt and pepper

1 Wash and dry the sardines and arrange on a grill pan.

2 To make the pesto, put the basil leaves, garlic and pine kernels in a food processor. Blend until finely chopped. Scrape out of the food processor and stir in the Parmesan and oil. Season to taste.

3 Spread a little of the pesto over one side of the sardines and place under a preheated hot grill for 3 minutes. Turn the fish, spread with more pesto, and grill for a further 3 minutes, or until the sardines are cooked through and the pesto is bubbling and beginning to brown.

4 Serve immediately with extra pesto and lemon wedges.

Pasta Puttanesca

The story goes that this is a dish made and eaten by Italian prostitutes who needed a quick and simple meal to keep them going.

NUTRITIONAL INFORMATION

Calories	359	Sugars	.......10g
Protein	.......10g	Fat	..........14g
Carbohydrate	..51g	Saturates	......2g

10 mins   25 mins

SERVES 4

INGREDIENTS

3 tbsp extra-virgin olive oil

1 large red onion, finely chopped

4 anchovy fillets, drained

pinch chilli flakes

2 garlic cloves, finely chopped

400 g/14 oz canned chopped tomatoes

2 tbsp tomato purée

225 g/8 oz dried spaghetti

25 g/1 oz pitted black olives, roughly chopped

25 g/1 oz pitted green olives, roughly chopped

1 tbsp capers, drained and rinsed

4 sun-dried tomatoes, roughly chopped

salt and pepper

1 Heat the oil in a saucepan and add the onion, anchovies and chilli flakes. Cook for 10 minutes, or until softened and starting to brown. Add the garlic and cook for 30 seconds.

2 Add the tomatoes and purée and bring to the boil. Simmer for 10 minutes.

3 Meanwhile, cook the spaghetti in plenty of boiling salted water according to the packet instructions until tender but still firm to the bite.

4 Add the olives, capers and sun-dried tomatoes to the sauce. Simmer for a further 2–3 minutes. Season to taste.

5 Drain the pasta well and stir in the sauce. Toss well to mix. Serve immediately.

Spinach & Onion Frittata

This Italian version of a flat omelette filled with spring onions, spinach and herbs, is finished under a hot grill.

NUTRITIONAL INFORMATION

Calories 145	Sugars 0.1g
Protein 8g	Fat 12g
Carbohydrate ... 1g	Saturates 3g

10 mins, plus 5 mins standing

15 mins

SERVES 6–8

I N G R E D I E N T S

4 tbsp olive oil

6 spring onions, sliced

250 g/9 oz young spinach leaves, any coarse stems removed, rinse

6 large eggs

3 tbsp finely chopped mixed fresh herbs, such as flat-leaved parsley, thyme and coriander

2 tbsp freshly grated Parmesan cheese, plus extra for garnishing

salt and pepper

fresh parsley sprigs, to garnish

1 Heat a 25 cm/10 inch frying pan, preferably a non-stick one with a flameproof handle, over a medium heat. Add the oil and heat. Add the spring onions and fry for about 2 minutes. Add the spinach with only the water clinging to its leaves, then cook until it wilts.

2 Beat the eggs together in a large bowl and season generously with salt and pepper. Using a slotted spoon, transfer the spinach and onions from the pan to the bowl of eggs and stir in the herbs. Pour the excess oil left in the frying pan into a heat-proof jug, then scrape off the crusty bits from the base of the pan.

3 Reheat the pan. Add 2 tablespoons of the reserved oil. Pour in the egg mixture, smoothing it into an even layer. Cook for 6 minutes, shaking the pan occasionally, or until the base is set when you lift up the side with a spatula.

4 Sprinkle the top of the frittata with the Parmesan cheese. Place the pan below a preheated grill and cook for 3 minutes, or until the excess liquid is set and the cheese has turned golden.

5 Remove the pan from the heat and slide the frittata on to a serving plate. Leave to stand for at least 5 minutes before serving, garnished with extra Parmesan and parsley. Serve hot or warm.

Spanakopittas

These Greek spinach and feta pies, with layers of crisp filo pastry, are often made in one large pan, but individual ones make a good starter.

NUTRITIONAL INFORMATION

Calories	 952	Sugars	.... 15g
Protein	.... 18g	Fat	.... 61g
Carbohydrate	.. 87g	Saturates	..... 29g

🥄 25 mins, plus 5 mins standing   🕐 25 mins

SERVES 4

INGREDIENTS

2 tbsp olive oil

6 spring onions, chopped

250 g/9 oz fresh young spinach leaves, tough stems removed, rinsed

60 g/2 oz long-grain rice (not basmati), boiled until tender and drained

4 tbsp chopped fresh dill

4 tbsp chopped fresh parsley

4 tbsp pine kernels

2 tbsp raisins

60 g/2¼ oz feta cheese, drained if necessary and crumbled

1¼ nutmeg, freshly grated

pinch of cayenne pepper (optional)

40 sheets filo pastry

250 g/9 oz melted butter

pepper

2 Stir in the rice, herbs, pine kernels, raisins, feta cheese and nutmeg, and add black and cayenne peppers to taste.

3 Leave the filo sheets in a stack. Cut forty 15 cm/6 inch squares. Remove 8 slices and cut into eight 10 cm/4 inch circles. Re-wrap the unused pastry and cover the squares and circles with a damp tea towel.

4 Brush four 10 cm/4 inch loose-bottomed tart tins with melted butter. Lay in one square of filo across a tin and brush with melted butter. Repeat the same process with 9 more sheets. Do not push the filo into the ridges.

5 Spoon in one-quarter of the filling and smooth the surface. Top with a filo circle and brush with butter. Repeat with another filo circle. Fold the over-hanging filo over the top and brush with butter. Repeat to make 3 more pies.

6 Put the pies on a baking sheet and bake in a preheated oven at 180°C/350°F/Gas Mark 4 for 20–25 minutes, or until crisp and golden. Leave to stand for about 5 minutes before turning out.

1 Heat the oil in a saucepan, add the spring onions and fry for about 2 minutes. Add the spinach, with just the water clinging to the leaves, and cook, stirring, until the leaves wilt. Transfer the spinach and onions to a bowl and, when cool enough to handle, squeeze out and drain off all the liquid.

Pan Bagna

A cornucopia of the best flavours of the Mediterranean, this French
sandwich never follows a set recipe. Treat this version as a suggestion.

NUTRITIONAL INFORMATION

Calories 422	Sugars 4g
Protein 27g	Fat 16g
Carbohydrate ..44g	Saturates 3g

15 mins, plus
3 hrs chilling

0 mins

SERVES 4

INGREDIENTS

40 cm/16 inch long loaf of country bread,
thicker than a French baguette

fruity extra-virgin olive oil

Black or Green Olive Tapenade
(see page 12) (optional)

FILLING

2 eggs, hard-boiled and shelled

50 g/1¾ oz anchovy fillets in oil

about 85 g/3 oz flavoured olives of your
choice

lettuce or rocket leaves, rinsed and patted
dry

about 4 plum tomatoes, sliced

200 g/7 oz canned tuna in brine, well
drained and flaked

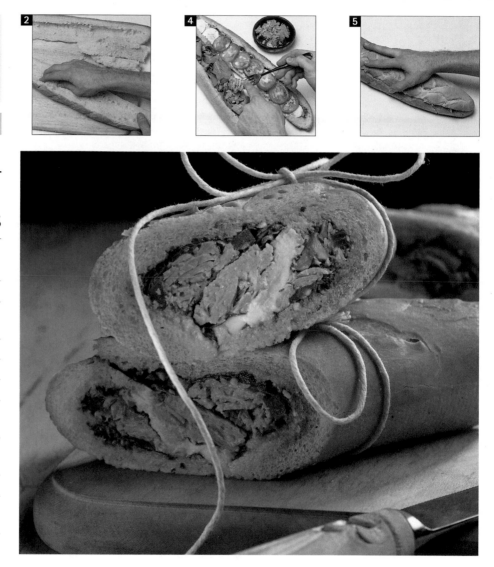

1 Slice the eggs. Drain the anchovy
fillets, then cut in half lengthways.
Stone the olives and slice in half.

2 Slice the loaf in half lengthways. Pull
out about 1 cm/½ inch of the crumb
from the top and bottom, leaving a border
all around both halves.

3 Generously brush both halves with
olive oil. Spread with tapenade, if you
like a strong flavour. Arrange lettuce or
rocket leaves on the bottom half.

4 Add layers of hard-boiled egg slices,
tomato slices, olives, anchovies and
tuna, sprinkling with olive oil and adding
lettuce or rocket leaves between the layers.
Make the filling as thick as you like.

5 Place the other bread half on top and
press down firmly. Wrap tightly in
cling film and place on a board or plate
that will fit in your refrigerator. Weight
down and chill for several hours. To serve,
slice into 4 equal portions, tying with string
to secure in place, if wished.

VARIATION
Other typical Mediterranean fillings for
a Pan Bagna include crushed garlic, red
or green peppers, young broad beans,
gherkins, artichoke hearts, Spanish
onion and pitted olives.

Baked Aubergine Gratin

Serve as an accompaniment to lamb, or as a vegetarian meal with plenty of French bread.

NUTRITIONAL INFORMATION

Calories 261   Sugars 5g
Protein . . . . 20g   Fat 18g
Carbohydrate . . . 6g   Saturates 10g

15 mins, plus
30 mins draining   40 mins

SERVES 4–6

INGREDIENTS

1 large aubergine, about 800 g/1 lb 12 oz

salt

300 g/10½ oz mozzarella cheese

85 g/3 oz Parmesan cheese

olive oil

250 ml/9 fl oz good-quality bottled tomato sauce for pasta

salt and pepper

1 Top and tail the aubergine and, using a sharp knife, cut into 5 mm/¼ inch slices crossways. Arrange the slices on a large plate, sprinkle with salt and set aside for 30 minutes to drain.

2 Meanwhile, drain and grate the mozzarella cheese and finely grate the Parmesan cheese. Set aside.

3 Rinse the aubergine slices and pat dry with paper towels. Lightly brush a baking sheet with olive oil and arrange the aubergine slices in a single layer. Brush the tops with olive oil.

4 Roast in a preheated oven at 200°C/ 400°F/Gas Mark 6 for 5 minutes. Turn the slices, brush with a little more oil and bake for a further 5 minutes, or until cooked through and tender. Do not turn off the oven.

5 Spread about 1 tablespoon olive oil in a gratin dish. Add a layer of aubergine slices, about a quarter of the tomato sauce and a quarter of the mozzarella. Season to taste with salt and pepper.

6 Continue layering until all the ingredients are used, ending with a layer of sauce. Sprinkle the Parmesan over the top. Bake in the oven for 30 minutes, or until bubbling.

COOK'S TIP
The aubergine slices are salted, or 'degorged', in order to get rid of any bitter juices.

Char-grilled Vegetables

This medley of peppers, courgettes, aubergine and red onion can be served on its own or as an unusual side dish.

NUTRITIONAL INFORMATION

Calories 66	Sugars 7g
Protein 2g	Fat 3g
Carbohydrate . . . 7g	Saturates 0.5g

15 mins   15 mins

SERVES 4

I N G R E D I E N T S

1 large red pepper

1 large green pepper

1 large orange pepper

1 large courgette

4 baby aubergines

2 medium red onions

2 tbsp lemon juice

1 tbsp olive oil

1 garlic clove, crushed

1 tbsp chopped fresh rosemary or 1 tsp dried rosemary

salt and pepper

TO SERVE

cracked wheat, cooked

tomato and olive relish

1 Halve and deseed the peppers and cut them into even-sized pieces, each about 2.5 cm/1 inch wide.

2 Trim the courgettes, cut them in half lengthways and then slice into 2.5 cm/1 inch pieces.

3 Trim the aubergines and quarter them lengthways. Peel both the onions, then cut each one into 8 even-sized wedges.

4 Mix the aubergine, onions, peppers and courgettes in a large bowl.

5 In a small bowl, whisk together the lemon juice, olive oil, garlic, rosemary and seasoning. Pour over the vegetables and stir to coat evenly.

6 Preheat the grill to medium. Thread the vegetables on to 8 metal or pre-soaked wooden skewers. Arrange the kebabs on the rack and cook for 10–12 minutes, turning frequently until the vegetables are lightly charred and just softened.

7 Serve the vegetable kebabs on a bed of cracked wheat accompanied by a tomato and olive relish.

Spanish Tortilla

This classic Spanish dish is often served as part of a tapas (appetizer) selection. A variety of cooked vegetables can be added to this recipe.

NUTRITIONAL INFORMATION

Calories 430   Sugars 6g
Protein .... 16g   Fat 20g
Carbohydrate .. 50g   Saturates 4g

10 mins   35 mins

SERVES 4

I N G R E D I E N T S

1 kg/2 lb 4 oz waxy potatoes, thinly sliced

4 tbsp vegetable oil

1 onion, sliced

2 garlic cloves, crushed

1 green pepper, seeded and diced

2 tomatoes, deseeded and chopped

25 g/1 oz canned sweetcorn, drained

6 large eggs, beaten

2 tbsp chopped parsley

salt and pepper

1   Parboil the potatoes in a saucepan of lightly salted boiling water for 5 minutes. Drain well.

2   Heat the oil in a large frying pan, add the potato and onions and sauté over a low heat, stirring constantly, for 5 minutes, or until the potatoes have browned.

3   Add the garlic, diced pepper, chopped tomatoes and sweetcorn, mixing well.

4   Pour in the eggs and add the chopped parsley. Season well with salt and pepper. Cook for 10-12 minutes, or until the underside is cooked through.

5   Remove the frying pan from the heat and continue to cook the tortilla under a preheated medium grill for 5-7 minutes, or until the tortilla is set and the top is golden brown.

6   Cut the tortilla into wedges or cubes, depending on your preference, and transfer to serving dishes. In Spain, tortillas are served hot, cold or warm.

COOK'S TIP

Ensure that the handle of your pan is heatproof before placing it under the grill and be sure to use an oven glove when removing it as it will be very hot.

Olive, Pepper & Tomato Pasta

The sweet cherry tomatoes in this recipe add colour and flavour and are complemented by the black olives and peppers.

NUTRITIONAL INFORMATION

Calories ......361 Sugars 8g
Protein ....8g Fat 14g
Carbohydrate ..49g Saturates 5g

10 mins 20 mins

SERVES 4

INGREDIENTS

225 g/8 oz dried penne

2 tbsp olive oil

2 tbsp butter

2 garlic cloves, crushed

1 green pepper, thinly sliced

1 yellow pepper, thinly sliced

16 cherry tomatoes, halved

1 tbsp chopped oregano

125 ml/4 fl oz dry white wine

2 tbsp quartered, pitted black olives

75 g/2¾ oz rocket

salt and pepper

fresh oregano sprigs, to garnish

1 Cook the pasta in a saucepan of boiling salted water for 8–10 minutes, or until firm to the bite. Drain thoroughly.

2 Heat the oil and butter in a pan until the butter melts. Sauté the garlic for 30 seconds. Add the peppers and cook for 3–4 minutes, stirring.

3 Stir in the cherry tomatoes, oregano, wine and olives and cook for 3–4 minutes. Season well with salt and pepper and stir in the rocket until just wilted.

4 Transfer the pasta to a serving dish, spoon over the sauce and mix well. Garnish with the oregano sprigs and serve.

COOK'S TIP

Ensure that the saucepan is large enough to prevent the pasta strands from sticking together during cooking.

Spaghetti alla Carbonara

Ensure that all of the cooked ingredients are as hot as possible before adding the eggs, so that they cook on contact.

NUTRITIONAL INFORMATION

Calories	 1092	Sugars	.... 9g
Protein	.... 37g	Fat	.... 69g
Carbohydrate	.. 86g	Saturates	..... 36g

10 mins   15 mins

SERVES 4

INGREDIENTS

425 g/15 oz dried spaghetti

2 tbsp olive oil

1 large onion, thinly sliced

2 garlic cloves, chopped

175 g/6 oz rindless bacon, cut into thin strips

25 g/1 oz butter

175 g/6 oz mushrooms, thinly sliced

300 ml/10 fl oz double cream

3 eggs, beaten

100 g /3½ oz freshly grated Parmesan cheese, plus extra to serve (optional)

salt and pepper

fresh sage sprigs, to garnish

1 Warm a large serving dish or bowl. Bring a large pan of lightly salted water to the boil. Add the spaghetti and 1 tbsp of the oil and cook until tender, but still firm to the bite. Drain, return to the pan and keep warm.

2 Meanwhile, heat the remaining oil in a frying pan over a medium heat. Add the onion and fry until it is transparent. Add the garlic and bacon and fry until the bacon is crisp. Transfer to the warm plate.

3 Melt the butter in the frying pan. Add the mushrooms and fry, stirring occasionally, for 3-4 minutes. Return the bacon mixture to the pan. Cover and keep warm.

4 Mix together the cream, eggs and cheese in a large bowl and then season to taste with salt and pepper.

5 Working very quickly, tip the spaghetti into the bacon and mushroom mixture and pour over the eggs. Toss the spaghetti quickly into the egg and cream mixture, using 2 forks, and serve immediately, garnished with sage sprigs. If you wish, serve with extra grated Parmesan cheese.

COOK'S TIP

The key to success with this recipe is not to overcook the egg. That is why it is important to keep all the ingredients hot enough just to cook the egg and to work rapidly to avoid scrambling it.

Pasta with Bacon & Tomatoes

As this dish cooks, the mouthwatering aroma of bacon, sweet tomatoes and oregano is a feast in itself.

NUTRITIONAL INFORMATION

Calories 431   Sugars 8g
Protein .... 10g   Fat 29g
Carbohydrate .. 34g   Saturates 14g

🥖 🥖 🥖

🍲 10 mins   🕐 25 mins

SERVES 4

I N G R E D I E N T S

900 g/2 lb small, sweet tomatoes

6 slices rindless smoked bacon

60 g/2¼ oz butter

1 onion, chopped

1 garlic clove, crushed

4 fresh oregano sprigs, finely chopped

450 g/1 lb dried orecchiette

1 tbsp olive oil

salt and pepper

freshly grated pecorino cheese, to serve

1 Blanch the tomatoes in boiling water. Drain, skin and seed the tomatoes, then roughly chop the flesh.

2 Using a sharp knife, chop the bacon into small dice.

3 Melt the butter in a saucepan. Add the bacon and fry until it is golden.

4 Add the onion and garlic and fry over a medium heat until just softened.

5 Add the tomatoes and oregano to the pan and then season to taste with salt and pepper. Lower the heat and simmer for 10-12 minutes.

6 Meanwhile, bring a large pan of lightly salted water to the boil. Add the orecchiette and oil and cook for 12 minutes, or until just tender, but still firm to the bite. Drain the pasta and transfer to a warm serving dish or bowl.

7 Spoon the bacon and tomato sauce over the pasta, toss to coat and serve with the cheese.

Tagliarini with Gorgonzola

This simple, creamy pasta sauce is a classic Italian recipe. You could use Danish blue cheese instead of the Gorgonzola, if you prefer.

NUTRITIONAL INFORMATION

Calories 904	Sugars 4g	
Protein 27g	Fat 53g	
Carbohydrate .. 83g	Saturates 36g	

10 mins   15 mins

SERVES 4

INGREDIENTS

25 g/1 oz butter

225 g/8 oz Gorgonzola cheese, roughly crumbled

150 ml/5 fl oz double cream

2 tbsp dry white wine

1 tsp cornflour

4 fresh sage sprigs, finely chopped

400 g/14 oz dried tagliarini

2 tbsp olive oil

salt and white pepper

1 Melt the butter in a heavy-based pan. Stir in 175 g/6 oz of the cheese and melt, over a low heat, for about 2 minutes.

2 Add the double cream, wine and cornflour and beat with a whisk until fully incorporated.

COOK'S TIP

Gorgonzola is one of the world's oldest veined cheeses and, arguably, its finest. When buying, always check that it is creamy yellow with delicate green veining. Avoid hard or discoloured cheese. It should have a rich, piquant aroma, not a bitter smell.

3 Stir in the sage and season to taste with salt and white pepper. Bring to the boil over a low heat, whisking constantly, until the sauce thickens. Remove from the heat and set aside while you cook the pasta.

4 Bring a large saucepan of lightly salted water to the boil. Add the tagliarini and 1 tbsp of the olive oil. Cook the pasta for 8–10 minutes, or until just tender, then drain thoroughly and toss in the remaining olive oil. Transfer the pasta to a serving dish and keep warm.

5 Reheat the sauce over a low heat, whisking constantly. Spoon the Gorgonzola sauce over the tagliarini, generously sprinkle over the remaining cheese and serve immediately.

Baked Fennel Gratinati

Fennel is a common ingredient in Italian cooking. In this dish its distinctive flavour is offset by the smooth béchamel sauce.

NUTRITIONAL INFORMATION

Calories ...... 426 Sugars 9g
Protein .... 13g Fat 35g
Carbohydrate .. 16g Saturates 19g

🍞 🍞

🥘 10 mins   🕐 45 mins

SERVES 4

INGREDIENTS

4 heads fennel

25 g/1 oz butter

150 ml/5 fl oz dry white wine

⅓ quantity béchamel sauce (see page 40), enriched with 2 egg yolks

25 g/1 oz fresh white breadcrumbs

3 tbsp freshly grated Parmesan

salt and pepper

fennel fronds, to garnish

1 Remove any bruised or tough outer stalks of fennel and cut each head in half. Put into a saucepan of boiling salted water and simmer for 20 minutes, or until tender, then drain.

2 Butter an ovenproof dish liberally and arrange the drained fennel in it.

3 Mix the wine into the béchamel sauce and season with salt and pepper to taste. Pour over the fennel.

4 Sprinkle evenly with the breadcrumbs and then the Parmesan.

5 Place in a preheated oven, 200°C/ 400°F/Gas Mark 6, and then bake for 20 minutes, or until the top is golden. Serve garnished with fennel fronds.

Mediterranean Peppers

Serve the peppers with their tops for an attractive finish – blanch them with the peppers, then bake separately for the last 10 minutes.

NUTRITIONAL INFORMATION

Calories 366   Sugars 24g
Protein . . . . 12g   Fat 12g
Carbohydrate . . 54g   Saturates 4g

1hr 10 mins   20 mins

SERVES 6

INGREDIENTS

6 large peppers, red, yellow and orange

200 g/7 oz long-grain white rice

2–3 tbsp olive oil, plus extra for greasing and drizzling

1 large onion

2 celery sticks, chopped

2 garlic cloves, finely chopped

½ tsp ground cinnamon or allspice

75 g/2¾ oz raisins

4 tbsp pine kernels, lightly toasted

4 ripe plum tomatoes, deseeded and chopped

50 ml/2 fl oz white wine

4 anchovy fillets, chopped

½ bunch chopped fresh parsley

½ bunch chopped fresh mint

6 tbsp freshly grated Parmesan cheese

salt and pepper

fresh tomato sauce, to serve (optional)

1 Using a sharp knife, slice off the tops of the peppers, then remove the cores and seeds. Blanch the peppers in boiling water for 2–3 minutes. Carefully remove and drain upside-down on a wire rack.

2 Cook the rice in boiling salted water until tender, but firm to the bite. Drain and rinse under cold running water.

3 Heat the oil in a large frying pan. Add the onion and celery and then cook for 2 minutes. Stir in the garlic, cinnamon and raisins and cook for 1 minute. Fork in the rice, then stir in the pine kernels, tomatoes, wine, anchovies, parsley and mint and cook for 4 minutes. Remove from the heat, add salt and pepper to taste and stir in half the Parmesan cheese.

4 Brush the bottom of a baking dish with a little oil. Divide the rice mixture equally among the peppers. Arrange in the dish and sprinkle with the remaining Parmesan. Drizzle with a little more oil and pour in enough water to come 1 cm/½ inch up the sides of the peppers. Loosely cover the dish with kitchen foil.

5 Bake in a preheated oven at 180°C/ 350°F/Gas Mark 4 for about 40 minutes. Uncover and cook for a further 10 minutes. Serve hot with tomato sauce.

Veal Chops with Salsa Verde

This vibrant green Italian sauce adds a touch of Mediterranean flavour to any simply cooked meat or seafood.

NUTRITIONAL INFORMATION

Calories ...... 481 Sugars 1g
Protein .... 41g Fat 34g
Carbohydrate ... 2g Saturates 5g

10 mins   5 mins

SERVES 4

INGREDIENTS

4 veal chops, such as loin chops, about 225 g/8 oz each and 2 cm/¾ inch thick

garlic-flavoured olive oil, for brushing

salt and pepper

fresh basil or oregano leaves, to garnish

SALSA VERDE

60 g/2¼ oz fresh flat-leaved parsley leaves

3 canned anchovy fillets in oil, drained

½ tbsp capers in brine, rinsed and drained

1 shallot, finely chopped

1 garlic clove, halved, green core removed and chopped

1 tbsp lemon juice, or to taste

6 large fresh basil leaves, or ¾ tsp freeze-dried

2 sprigs fresh oregano, or ½ tsp dried

125 ml/4 fl oz extra-virgin olive oil

1 To make the salsa verde, put all the ingredients, except the olive oil, in a blender or food processor and process until they are chopped and blended.

2 With the motor running, add the oil through the top or feed tube and quickly blend until thickened. Add pepper to taste. Transfer to a bowl, cover and chill.

3 Lightly brush the veal chops with olive oil and season them with salt and pepper. Place under a preheated grill and cook for about 3 minutes. Turn over, brush with more oil and grill for a further 2 minutes, or until cooked when tested with the tip of a knife.

4 Transfer the chops to individual plates and spoon a little of the chilled salsa verde alongside them. Garnish the chops with fresh oregano or basil and serve with the remaining salsa verde.

COOK'S TIP

The salsa verde will keep for up to 2 days in a covered container in the refrigerator. It is also fantastic served with grilled red mullet.

Spanish Chicken with Garlic

The slow cooking takes all the harsh flavour out of the garlic cloves and makes them tender in this simple dish.

NUTRITIONAL INFORMATION

Calories 496	Sugars 1g
Protein 41g	Fat 22g
Carbohydrate .. 15g	Saturates 5g

🍗 🍗 🍗

🍲 10 mins   🕐 45 mins

SERVES 4

I N G R E D I E N T S

2–3 tbsp plain flour

cayenne pepper

4 chicken quarters or other joints, patted dry

about 4 tbsp olive oil

20 large garlic cloves, each halved and
    green core removed

1 large bay leaf

450 ml/16 fl oz chicken stock

4 tbsp dry white wine

chopped fresh parsley, to garnish

salt and pepper

1 Put about 2 tablespoons of the flour in a bag and season to taste with cayenne pepper and salt and pepper. Add a chicken piece and shake until it is lightly coated with the flour, shaking off the excess. Repeat with the remaining pieces, adding more flour and seasoning, if necessary.

2 Heat 3 tablespoons of the olive oil in a large frying pan. Add the garlic cloves and fry for about 2 minutes, stirring, to flavour the oil. Remove with a slotted spoon and set aside.

3 Add the chicken pieces to the pan, skin-side down, and fry for 5 minutes, or until the skin is golden brown. Turn and fry for a further 5 minutes, adding an extra 1–2 tablespoons oil if necessary.

4 Return the garlic to the pan. Add the bay leaf, chicken stock and wine and bring to the boil. Lower the heat, cover and simmer for 25 minutes, or until the chicken is tender and the garlic cloves are very soft.

5 Using a slotted spoon, transfer the chicken to a serving platter and keep warm. Bring the cooking liquid to the boil, with the garlic, and boil until reduced to about 250 ml/ 9 fl oz. Adjust the seasoning, if necessary.

6 Spoon the sauce over the chicken pieces and scatter the garlic cloves around. Garnish with parsley and serve.

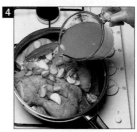

COOK'S TIP

The cooked garlic cloves are delicious mashed into a purée on the side of the plate for smearing on the chicken pieces.

Basque Pork & Beans

Dried cannellini beans feature in many Italian, Spanish, French and Greek stews and casseroles, especially during the winter.

NUTRITIONAL INFORMATION

Calories	240	Sugars	6g
Protein	30g	Fat	4g
Carbohydrate	23g	Saturates	1g

12 hrs soaking, plus 20 mins   1hr 40 mins

SERVES 4–6

INGREDIENTS

200 g/7 oz dried cannellini beans, soaked overnight

olive oil

600 g/1 lb 5 oz boneless leg of pork, cut into 5 cm/2 inch chunks

1 large onion, sliced

3 large garlic cloves, crushed

400 g/14 oz canned chopped tomatoes

2 green peppers, cored, deseeded and sliced

finely grated rind of 1 large orange

salt and pepper

finely chopped fresh parsley, to garnish

1 Drain the cannellini beans and put in a large saucepan with fresh water to cover. Bring to the boil and boil rapidly for 10 minutes. Lower the heat and simmer for 20 minutes. Drain and set aside.

2 Add enough oil to cover the base of a large frying pan in a very thin layer. Heat the oil over a medium heat, add a few pieces of the pork to the pan and fry on all sides until the pork is evenly browned on all sides. Repeat with the remaining pork and set aside.

3 Add 1 tablespoon oil to the frying pan, if necessary, then add the onion and fry for 3 minutes. Stir in the garlic and fry for a further 2 minutes. Return the browned pork to the frying pan.

4 Add the tomatoes to the pan and bring to the boil. Lower the heat, then stir in the pepper slices, orange rind, the drained beans and salt and pepper to taste.

5 Transfer the contents of the pan, including the juices, to a casserole.

6 Cover the casserole and cook in a preheated oven at 180°C/350°F/Gas Mark 4 for 45 minutes, or until the beans and pork are tender. Sprinkle with parsley and serve at once.

VARIATIONS

Any leftover beans and peppers can be used as a pasta sauce. Add sliced and fried chorizo sausage for a spicier dish.

Veal Italienne

This dish is really superb if made with tender veal. However, if veal is unavailable, use pork or turkey escalopes instead.

NUTRITIONAL INFORMATION

Calories 592	Sugars 5g
Protein 44g	Fat 23g
Carbohydrate .. 48g	Saturates 9g

15 mins   1 hr 20 mins

SERVES 4

INGREDIENTS

60 g/2¼ oz butter

1 tbsp olive oil

675 g/1½ lb potatoes, cubed

4 veal escalopes, weighing 175 g/6 oz each

1 onion, cut into 8 wedges

2 garlic cloves, crushed

2 tbsp plain flour

2 tbsp tomato purée

150 ml/5 fl oz red wine

300 ml/10 fl oz chicken stock

8 ripe tomatoes, peeled, seeded and diced

25 g/1 oz stoned black olives, halved

2 tbsp chopped fresh basil

salt and pepper

fresh basil leaves, to garnish

1 Heat the butter and oil in a large frying pan. Add the potato cubes and cook for 5-7 minutes, stirring frequently, until they begin to brown.

2 Remove the browned potatoes from the pan with a perforated spoon and set them aside.

3 Place the veal escalopes in the frying pan and cook for just 2-3 minutes on each side until sealed. Remove from the pan and set aside.

4 Stir the onion and garlic into the pan and cook for 2-3 minutes.

5 Add the flour and the tomato purée and cook for 1 minute, stirring. Gradually blend in the red wine and chicken stock, stirring thoroughly to make a smooth sauce.

6 Return the potatoes and veal to the pan. Stir in the tomatoes, olives and chopped basil and season with salt and pepper to taste.

7 Transfer to a casserole dish and cook in a preheated oven, 180°C/350°F/Gas Mark 4, for 1 hour or until the potatoes and veal are cooked through. Garnish with basil leaves and serve.

COOK'S TIP

For a quicker cooking time and really tender meat, pound the meat with a meat mallet to flatten it slightly before cooking.

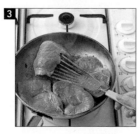

Fresh Spaghetti & Meatballs

This well-loved Italian dish is famous across the world. Make the most of it by using high-quality steak for the meatballs.

NUTRITIONAL INFORMATION

Calories	665	Sugars	9g
Protein	39g	Fat	24g
Carbohydrate	77g	Saturates	8g

🐻 🐻 🐻

30 mins soaking, plus 15mins   1 hr 10 mins

SERVES 4

INGREDIENTS

150 g/5½ oz brown breadcrumbs

150 ml/5 fl oz milk

25 g/1 oz butter

25 g/1 oz wholemeal flour

200 ml/7 fl oz beef stock

400 g/14 oz canned chopped tomatoes

2 tbsp tomato purée

1 tsp sugar

1 tbsp finely chopped fresh tarragon

1 large onion, finely chopped

450 g/1 lb minced steak

1 tsp paprika

4 tbsp olive oil

450 g/1 lb fresh spaghetti

salt and pepper

fresh tarragon sprigs, to garnish

1 Place the breadcrumbs in a bowl, then add the milk and set aside to soak for about 30 minutes.

2 Melt half of the butter in a pan. Add the flour and cook, stirring constantly, for 2 minutes. Gradually stir in the beef stock and cook, stirring constantly, for a further 5 minutes. Add the tomatoes, tomato purée, sugar and tarragon. Season well and simmer for 25 minutes.

3 Mix the onion, steak and paprika into the breadcrumbs and season to taste. Shape the mixture into 14 meatballs.

4 Heat the oil and remaining butter in a frying pan and fry the meatballs, turning, until brown all over. Place in a deep casserole, pour over the tomato sauce, cover and bake in a preheated oven, at 180°C/350°F/Gas Mark 4, for 25 minutes, or until the meatballs are cooked.

5 Bring a large saucepan of lightly salted water to the boil. Add the fresh spaghetti, bring back to the boil and cook for about 2–3 minutes, or until tender, but still firm to the bite.

6 Meanwhile, remove the meatballs from the oven and allow them to cool for 3 minutes. Serve the meatballs and their sauce with the spaghetti, garnished with tarragon sprigs.

Lasagne Verde

Today you can buy precooked lasagne sheets from most supermarkets; otherwise, prepare the sheets according to the packet instructions.

NUTRITIONAL INFORMATION

Calories 597   Sugars 12g
Protein .... 33g   Fat 27g
Carbohydrate .. 55g   Saturates 12g

🕒 25 mins   🕐 1³/₄ hrs

SERVES 4–6

INGREDIENTS

butter, for greasing

14 sheets pre-cooked lasagne

75 g/3 oz grated mozzarella cheese

salt and pepper

MEAT SAUCE

30 ml/1 fl oz olive oil

450 g/1 lb minced beef

1 large onion, chopped

1 celery stick, diced

4 cloves garlic, crushed

25g/1 oz plain flour

300 ml/10 fl oz beef stock

150 ml/5 fl oz red wine

1 tbsp chopped fresh parsley

1 tsp each chopped fresh marjoram and basil

2 tbsp tomato purée

BECHAMEL SAUCE

85 g/3 oz butter

85 g/3 oz plain flour

850 ml/1½ pints milk

2 tbsp finely chopped onion

2 parsley sprigs

pinch each dried thyme and nutmeg

1 To make the meat sauce, heat the olive oil in a large frying pan. Add the minced beef and fry until browned all over. Add the onion, celery and garlic and cook for 3 minutes.

2 Sprinkle over the flour and cook, stirring, for 1 minute. Gradually stir in the stock and red wine, season well and add the herbs. Bring to the boil, then simmer for 35 minutes. Add the tomato purée and simmer for 10 minutes.

3 To make the bechamel sauce, melt the butter in a saucepan, add the flour and cook for 2 minutes, stirring. Gradually stir in the milk. Add the remaining ingredients. Bring to the boil, stirring, then simmer for 15 minutes. Season to taste, then strain.

4 Lightly grease an ovenproof dish with butter. Arrange sheets of lasagne over the base of the dish, and spoon over a layer of meat sauce, then béchamel sauce. Repeat the process twice, finishing with a layer of béchamel sauce. Sprinkle over the grated mozzarella cheese.

5 Bake the lasagne in a preheated oven at 190°C/375°F/ Gas 5 for 35 minutes, or until the top is golden brown and bubbling. Serve immediately.

Pasticcio

A recipe that has both Italian and Greek origins, this dish may be served hot or cold, cut into thick, satisfying squares.

NUTRITIONAL INFORMATION

Calories	590	Sugars	8g
Protein	34g	Fat	39g
Carbohydrate	23g	Saturates	16g

25 mins   1 hrs 5 mins

SERVES 6

I N G R E D I E N T S

225 g/8 oz fusilli, or other short pasta shapes

1 tbsp olive oil

4 tbsp double cream

salt

rosemary sprigs, to garnish

S A U C E

2 tbsp olive oil, plus extra for brushing

1 onion, thinly sliced

1 red pepper, deseeded and chopped

2 garlic cloves, chopped

625 g/1 lb 6 oz lean minced beef

400 g/14 oz canned chopped tomatoes

125 ml/4 fl oz dry white wine

2 tbsp chopped fresh parsley

50 g/1¾ oz canned anchovies, drained and chopped

salt and pepper

T O P P I N G

300 ml/10 fl oz natural yogurt

3 eggs

pinch of freshly grated nutmeg

40 g/1½ oz Parmesan cheese, freshly grated

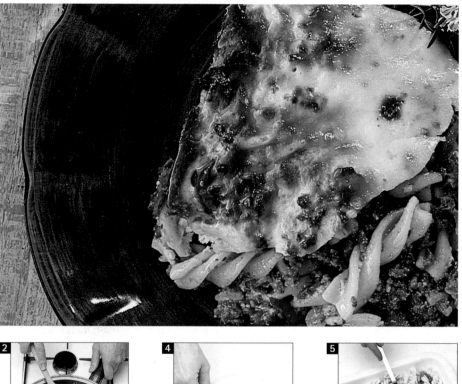

1 To make the sauce, heat the oil in a large frying pan and fry the onion and red pepper for 3 minutes. Stir in the garlic and cook for 1 minute more. Stir in the beef and cook, stirring frequently, until it is no longer pink.

2 Add the tomatoes and wine, stir well and bring to the boil. Simmer, uncovered, for 20 minutes, or until the sauce is fairly thick. Stir in the parsley and anchovies and season to taste.

3 Cook the pasta in a large pan of boiling salted water, adding the oil, for 8–10 minutes, or until tender. Drain the pasta in a colander, then transfer to a bowl. Stir in the cream and set aside.

4 To make the topping, beat together the yogurt, eggs and nutmeg until well combined and season with salt and pepper to taste.

5 Brush a large, shallow ovenproof dish with oil. Spoon in half of the pasta mixture and cover with half of the meat sauce. Repeat these layers, then spread the topping evenly over the final layer. Sprinkle the grated Parmesan cheese evenly on top.

6 Bake in a preheated oven, 190°C/ 375°F/Gas Mark 5, for 25 minutes, or until the topping is golden brown and bubbling. Garnish with sprigs of fresh rosemary and serve immediately.

Neapolitan Veal Cutlets

The delicious combination of apple, onion and mushroom perfectly complements the delicate flavour of veal.

NUTRITIONAL INFORMATION

Calories	1071	Sugars	13g
Protein	74g	Fat	59g
Carbohydrate	66g	Saturates	16g

20 mins   45 mins

SERVES 4

INGREDIENTS

200 g/7 oz butter

4 x 250 g/9 oz veal cutlets, trimmed

1 large onion, sliced

2 apples, peeled, cored and sliced

175 g/6 oz button mushrooms

1 tbsp chopped fresh tarragon

8 black peppercorns

1 tbsp sesame seeds

400 g/14 oz dried marille

100 ml/3½ fl oz extra virgin olive oil

2 large beef tomatoes, cut in half

175 g/6 oz mascarpone cheese

leaves of 1 fresh basil sprig

salt and pepper

fresh basil leaves, to garnish

1 Melt 60 g/2¼ oz of the butter in a frying pan. Fry the veal over a low heat for 5 minutes on each side. Keep warm.

2 Fry the onion and apples in the pan until lightly browned. Transfer to a dish, place the veal on top and keep warm.

3 Melt the remaining butter in the pan. Fry the mushrooms, tarragon and peppercorns over a low heat for 3 minutes. Sprinkle with the sesame seeds. Set aside.

4 Bring a pan of salted water to the boil. Add the pasta and 1 tbsp of oil. Cook for 8–10 minutes, or until tender, but still firm to the bite. Drain; transfer to a warmed ovenproof serving dish.

5 Grill the tomatoes for 2–3 minutes, or fry them in the frying pan.

6 Top the pasta with the mascarpone cheese and sprinkle over the remaining olive oil. Place the onions, apples and veal cutlets on top of the pasta. Spoon the mushrooms, peppercorns and pan juices on to the cutlets, place the tomatoes and basil leaves around the edge and place in a preheated oven at 150°C/300°F/Gas Mark 2 for 5 minutes.

7 Season to taste with salt and pepper, garnish with fresh basil leaves and serve immediately.

Pork with Ratatouille Sauce

Serve this delicious combination of meat and vegetables with baked potatoes for an appetizing supper dish.

NUTRITIONAL INFORMATION

Calories 230	Sugars 8g
Protein 29g	Fat 9g
Carbohydrate ... 8g	Saturates 3g

🔥

🥩 5 mins   🕐 35 mins

SERVES 4

I N G R E D I E N T S

4 lean, boneless pork chops, about 125 g/4½ oz each

1 tsp dried mixed herbs

salt and pepper

baked potatoes, to serve

S A U C E

1 medium onion

1 garlic clove

1 small green pepper, deseeded

1 small yellow pepper, deseeded

1 medium courgette, trimmed

100 g/3½ oz button mushrooms

400 g/14 oz canned chopped tomatoes

2 tbsp tomato purée

1 tsp dried mixed herbs

1 tsp caster sugar

1 To make the sauce, peel and chop the onion and garlic. Dice the peppers. Dice the courgette. Wipe and halve or slice the mushrooms.

2 Place all of the vegetables in a saucepan and stir in the canned chopped tomatoes and tomato purée. Add the dried herbs, sugar and plenty of seasoning. Bring the mixture to the boil, cover and simmer for 20 minutes.

3 Meanwhile, preheat the grill to medium. Trim away any excess fat from the chops, then season on both sides and rub in the dried mixed herbs. Cook the chops for 5 minutes, then turn over and cook for a further 6–7 minutes, or until cooked through.

4 Drain the chops on absorbent kitchen paper and serve accompanied by the sauce and baked potatoes.

COOK'S TIP

This vegetable sauce could be served with any other grilled or baked meat or fish.
It would also make an excellent vegetarian filling for savoury crêpes.

Pizzaiola Steak

This has a Neapolitan sauce, using the delicious red tomatoes so abundant in that area, but canned ones make an excellent alternative.

NUTRITIONAL INFORMATION

Calories	371	Sugars	7g
Protein	43g	Fat	19g
Carbohydrate	7g	Saturates	5g

🖐 🖐

🍲 25 mins   🕐 25 mins

SERVES 4

I N G R E D I E N T S

800 g/28 oz canned peeled tomatoes or 750 g/1 lb 10 oz fresh tomatoes

4 tbsp olive oil

2–3 garlic cloves, crushed

1 onion, chopped finely

1 tbsp tomato purée

1½ tsp chopped fresh marjoram or oregano or ¾ tsp dried marjoram or oregano

4 thin sirloin or rump steaks

2 tbsp chopped fresh parsley

1 tsp sugar

salt and pepper

fresh herbs, to garnish (optional)

sauté potatoes, to serve

1 If using canned tomatoes, purée them in a food processor, then sieve to remove the seeds. If using fresh tomatoes, loosen the skins by covering them with boiling water for 20 seconds, then peel, remove the seeds and chop finely.

2 Heat half of the oil in a pan and fry the garlic and onions very gently for about 5 minutes, or until softened.

3 Add the tomatoes, seasoning, tomato purée and chopped herbs to the pan. If using fresh tomatoes, add 4 tablespoons water too, and then simmer very gently for 8–10 minutes, giving an occasional stir.

4 Meanwhile, trim the steaks if necessary and season with salt and pepper. Heat the remaining oil in a frying pan and fry the steaks quickly on both sides to seal, then continue until cooked to your liking – 2 minutes for rare, 3–4 minutes for medium, or 5 minutes for well done. Alternatively, cook the steaks under a hot grill after brushing lightly with oil.

5 Adjust the seasoning of the sauce and stir in the chopped parsley and sugar.

6 Pour off the excess fat from the pan containing the steaks and add the tomato sauce. Reheat gently and serve at once, with the sauce spooned over and around the steaks. Garnish with sprigs of fresh herbs, if liked. Sauté potatoes and a green vegetable make very good accompaniments to this dish.

Stuffed Pork with Prosciutto

This sophisticated roast with Mediterranean flavours is ideal served with a pungent olive paste and a salad.

NUTRITIONAL INFORMATION

Calories 427	Sugars 0g	
Protein 31g	Fat 34g	
Carbohydrate ... 2g	Saturates 7g	

15 mins, plus 10 standing   40 mins

SERVES 4

I N G R E D I E N T S

500 g/1 lb 2 oz piece of lean pork fillet

small bunch fresh basil leaves, washed

2 tbsp freshly grated Parmesan

2 tbsp sun-dried tomato paste

6 thin slices Parma ham (prosciutto)

1 tbsp olive oil

salt and pepper

O L I V E   P A S T E

125 g/4½ oz pitted black olives

4 tbsp olive oil

2 garlic cloves, peeled

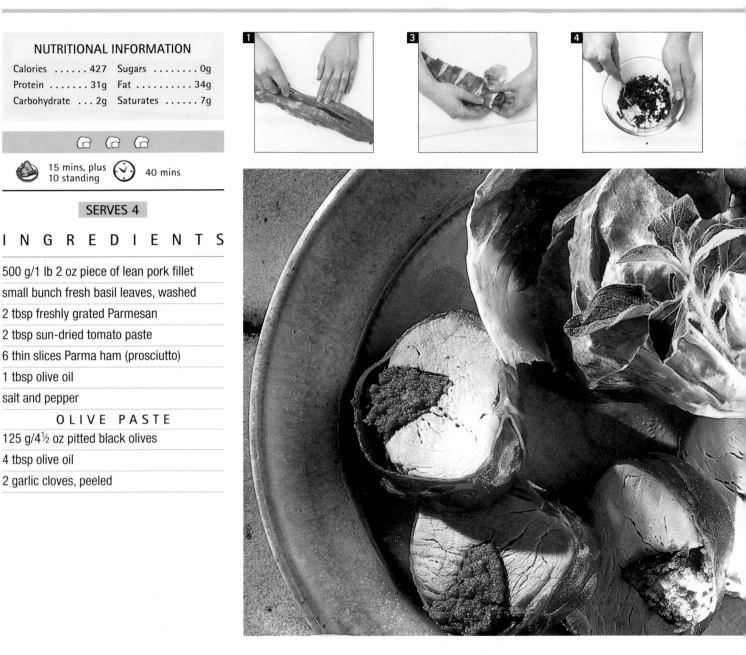

1 Trim away the excess fat and membrane from the pork fillet. Slice the pork lengthways down the middle, taking care not to cut all the way through.

2 Open out the pork and season the inside. Lay the basil leaves down the centre. Mix the cheese and sun-dried tomato paste and spread over the basil.

3 Press the pork fillet back together. Wrap the ham around the stuffed pork, overlapping it, to cover. Place it on a rack in a roasting tin, seamside down, and brush with oil. Bake in a preheated oven,190°C/375°F/Gas Mark 5, for 30–40 minutes depending on thickness, until cooked through. Allow the pork to stand for 10 minutes before serving.

4 To make the olive paste, place all the ingredients in a blender or a food processor and blend until smooth. For a coarser paste, finely chop the olives and garlic and mix with the oil.

5 Drain the cooked stuffed pork and slice it thinly. Serve it with the olive paste and an attractive salad.

Pork Chops with Sage

The fresh taste of sage is the perfect ingredient to counteract the richness of pork in this quick and simple dish.

NUTRITIONAL INFORMATION

Calories	 364	Sugars	.... 5g
Protein	.... 34g	Fat	.... 19g
Carbohydrate	.. 14g	Saturates	...... 7g

5 mins   20 mins

SERVES 4

INGREDIENTS

2 tbsp flour

1 tbsp chopped fresh sage or 1 tsp dried

4 lean boneless pork chops, trimmed of excess fat

2 tbsp olive oil

15 g/½ oz butter

2 red onions, sliced into rings

1 tbsp lemon juice

2 tsp caster sugar

4 plum tomatoes, quartered

salt and pepper

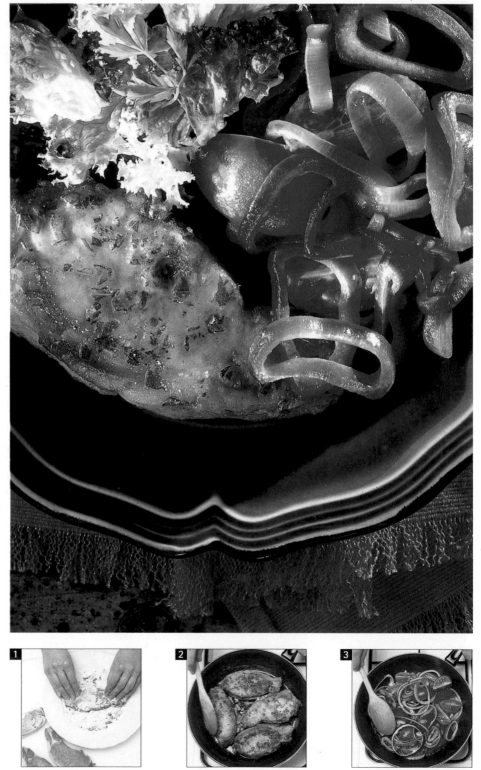

1 Mix the flour, sage and salt and pepper to taste on a plate. Lightly dust the pork chops on both sides with the seasoned flour.

2 Heat the oil and butter in a frying pan, then add the chops and cook them for 6–7 minutes on each side, or until cooked through. Drain the chops, reserving the pan juices, and keep warm.

3 Toss the onion in the lemon juice and fry along with the sugar and tomatoes for 5 minutes, or until tender.

4 Serve the pork with the tomato and onion mixture and a green salad.

Escalopes & Italian Sausage

Anchovies are often used to enhance flavour, particularly in meat dishes.
Either veal or turkey escalopes can be used for this pan-fried dish.

NUTRITIONAL INFORMATION

Calories 233	Sugars 1g	
Protein 28g	Fat 13g	
Carbohydrate ... 1g	Saturates 1g	

10 mins   20 mins

SERVES 4

INGREDIENTS

1 tbsp olive oil

6 canned anchovy fillets, drained

1 tbsp capers, drained

1 tbsp fresh rosemary, stalks removed

finely grated rind and juice of 1 orange

75 g/2¾ oz Italian sausage, diced

3 tomatoes, skinned and chopped

4 turkey or veal escalopes, each about
    125 g/4½ oz

salt and pepper

crusty bread or cooked polenta, to serve

1 Heat the oil in a large frying pan. Add the anchovies, capers, fresh rosemary, grated orange rind and juice, Italian sausage and tomatoes to the pan and cook for 5–6 minutes, stirring occasionally.

2 Meanwhile, place the turkey or veal escalopes between sheets of greaseproof paper. Pound the meat with a meat mallet or the end of a rolling pin in order to flatten it.

3 Add the escalopes to the mixture in the frying pan. Season to taste with salt and pepper, cover and cook for 3–5 minutes on each side, slightly longer if the meat is thicker.

4 Transfer to serving plates and serve with fresh crusty bread, or cooked polenta if you prefer.

VARIATION

Try using 4-minute steaks, slightly
flattened, instead of the turkey or veal.
Cook them for 4–5 minutes
on top of the sauce in the pan.

Sausage & Bean Casserole

In this easy-to-prepare traditional Tuscan dish, Italian sausages are cooked with cannellini beans and tomatoes.

NUTRITIONAL INFORMATION

Calories 609   Sugars 7g
Protein ....27g   Fat 47g
Carbohydrate ..20g   Saturates 16g

15 mins   30 mins

SERVES 4

INGREDIENTS

8 Italian sausages

1 tbsp olive oil

1 large onion, chopped

2 garlic cloves, chopped

1 green pepper

225g/8 oz fresh tomatoes, skinned and chopped or 400 g/14 oz canned tomatoes, chopped

2 tbsp sun-dried tomato paste

400 g/14 oz canned cannellini beans

mashed potato or rice, to serve

1 Using a sharp knife, deseed the pepper and cut it into thin strips.

2 Prick the sausages all over with a fork, then cook under a preheated grill, for 10–12 minutes, turning occasionally, until brown all over. Set aside and keep warm.

3 Heat the oil in a large frying pan. Add the onion, garlic and pepper and cook for 5 minutes, stirring occasionally.

4 Add the tomatoes and simmer for 5 minutes, stirring occasionally.

5 Stir in the sun-dried tomato paste, cannellini beans and sausages. Cook for 4–5 minutes, or until the mixture is piping hot. Add 4–5 tablespoons of water if the mixture becomes too dry.

6 Serve immediately with mashed potato or cooked rice.

COOK'S TIP

Italian sausages are coarse in texture and have quite a strong flavour. They can be bought in specialist sausage shops, Italian delicatessens and some larger supermarkets. They are replaceable in this recipe only by game sausages.

Sausage & Rosemary Risotto

This recipe is made with a mild Italian sausage called luganega, but you can use any sausage you like. A Spanish chorizo would add a robust flavour.

NUTRITIONAL INFORMATION

Calories 630   Sugars 4g
Protein .... 19g   Fat 34g
Carbohydrate .. 57g   Saturates 15g

20 mins   40 mins

SERVES 4–6

INGREDIENTS

2 long sprigs fresh rosemary, plus extra
  to garnish

2 tbsp olive oil

60 g/2¼ oz unsalted butter

1 large onion, finely chopped

1 celery stick, finely chopped

2 garlic cloves, finely chopped

½ tsp dried thyme leaves

450 g/1 lb pork sausage such as luganega
  or Cumberland, cut into
  1 cm/½ inch slices

350 g/12 oz arborio or carnaroli rice

125 ml/4 fl oz fruity red wine

1.3 litres/2¼ pints chicken stock, simmering

85 g/3 oz freshly grated Parmesan cheese

salt and pepper

1 Strip the long thin leaves from the rosemary sprigs and chop finely.

2 Heat the oil and half the butter in a large heavy-based saucepan over a medium heat. Add the onion and celery and cook for about 2 minutes. Stir in the garlic, thyme, sausage and rosemary. Cook for about 5 minutes, stirring frequently, until the sausage begins to brown. Transfer the sausage to a plate.

3 Stir the rice into the pan and cook, stirring, for about 2 minutes, or until the grains are translucent and well coated with the butter and oil.

4 Pour in the red wine; it will bubble and steam rapidly and evaporate almost immediately. Add a ladleful (about 225 ml/ 8 fl oz) of the simmering stock and cook, stirring, until it is all absorbed by the rice.

5 Continue adding the stock, about half a ladleful at a time, allowing each addition to be absorbed before adding the next. This should take 20–25 minutes. The risotto should have a creamy consistency and the rice should be tender, but firm to the bite.

6 Return the sausage pieces to the risotto and heat through. Remove from the heat; stir in the remaining butter and Parmesan. Season with salt and pepper. Cover, stand for about 1 minute, then garnish with rosemary and serve.

Mackerel Escabeche

Although *escabeche* – meaning 'pickled in vinegar' – is a Spanish word, variations of this dish are to be found all over the Mediterranean.

NUTRITIONAL INFORMATION

Calories	 750	Sugars	.... 3g
Protein	.... 33g	Fat	.... 63g
Carbohydrate	.. 12g	Saturates	..... 11g

15 mins   15 mins

SERVES 4

INGREDIENTS

150 ml/5 fl oz olive oil

4 mackerel, filleted

2 tbsp seasoned with salt and pepper, for dusting

4 tbsp red wine vinegar

1 onion, finely sliced

1 strip orange rind, removed with a potato peeler

1 sprig fresh thyme

1 sprig fresh rosemary

1 fresh bay leaf

4 garlic cloves, crushed

2 fresh red chillies, bruised

1 tsp salt

3 tbsp chopped fresh flat-leaved parsley

crusty bread, to serve

VARIATION

Substitute 12 whole sardines, cleaned, with heads removed. Cook in the same way. Tuna steaks are also very delicious served escabeche.

1 Heat half the olive oil in a frying pan and dust the mackerel fillets with the seasoned flour.

2 Add the fish to the frying pan and cook for 30 seconds on each side. The fish will not be cooked through.

3 Transfer the mackerel to a shallow dish, that is large enough to hold the fillets in one layer.

4 Add the the vinegar, sliced onion, strip of orange rind, thyme, rosemary, bay leaf, garlic, chillies and salt to the pan. Simmer for 10 minutes.

5 Add the remaining olive oil and the chopped parsley. Pour the mixture over the fish and leave until cold. Serve with plenty of crusty bread.

Cotriade

This is a rich French stew of fish and vegetables, flavoured with saffron and herbs. The fish and vegetables are served separately from the soup.

NUTRITIONAL INFORMATION

Calories	 81	Sugars	. . . . 0.9g
Protein	. . . . . . 7.4g	Fat	. . . . 3.9g
Carbohydrate	. . 3.8g	Saturates	. . . . . 1.1g

🕝 15 mins   🕐 45 mins

SERVES 6

I N G R E D I E N T S

large pinch saffron

600 ml/1 pint hot fish stock

1 tbsp olive oil

2 tbsp butter

1 onion, sliced

2 garlic cloves, chopped

1 leek, sliced

1 small fennel bulb, finely sliced

450 g/1 lb potatoes, cut into chunks

150 ml/5 fl oz dry white wine

1 tbsp fresh thyme leaves

2 bay leaves

4 ripe tomatoes, skinned and chopped

900g/2 lb mixed fish such as haddock, hake, mackerel, red or grey mullet

2 tbsp chopped fresh parsley

salt and pepper

crusty bread, to serve

1 Using a mortar and pestle, crush the saffron and add to the hot fish stock. Stir the mixture and leave to infuse for at least 10 minutes. Chop the fish roughly and set aside.

2 In a large saucepan, heat the oil and butter together. Add the onion and cook gently for 4–5 minutes, or until softened. Add the garlic, leek, fennel and potatoes. Cover and cook for a further 10–15 minutes, or until the vegetables are softened.

3 Add the wine and simmer rapidly for 3–4 minutes, or until reduced by half. Add the thyme, bay leaves and tomatoes and stir well. Add the saffron-infused fish stock. Bring to the boil, cover and simmer gently for 15 minutes, or until the vegetables are tender.

4 Add the fish, return to the boil and simmer for a further 3–4 minutes, or until all the fish is tender. Add the parsley and season to taste. Using a slotted spoon, remove the fish and vegetables to a warmed serving dish. Serve the soup with plenty of crusty bread.

VARIATION

Once the fish and vegetables have been cooked, you could process the soup and pass it through a sieve to give a smooth fish soup.

Moroccan Fish Tagine

A tagine is a Moroccan earthenware dish with a domed lid that has a steam hole in the top. However, you can use an ordinary saucepan.

NUTRITIONAL INFORMATION

Calories	 188	Sugars 5g
Protein	.... 17g	Fat 11g
Carbohydrate	... 7g	Saturates 1g

15 mins

1 hr 10 mins

SERVES 4

INGREDIENTS

2 tbsp olive oil

1 large onion, finely chopped

large pinch saffron strands

½ tsp ground cinnamon

1 tsp ground coriander

½ tsp ground cumin

½ tsp ground turmeric

200 g/7 oz canned chopped tomatoes

300 ml/10 fl oz fish stock

4 small red mullet cleaned, boned and heads and tails removed

50 g/1¾ oz pitted green olives

1 tbsp chopped preserved lemon

3 tbsp fresh chopped coriander

salt and pepper

couscous, to serve

1 Heat the olive oil in a large saucepan or flameproof casserole. Add the onion and cook gently for 10 minutes without colouring until softened. Add the saffron, cinnamon, coriander, cumin and turmeric and cook for a further 30 seconds, stirring.

2 Add the chopped tomatoes and fish stock and stir well. Bring to the boil, cover and simmer for 15 minutes. Uncover and simmer for a further 20–35 minutes, or until thickened.

3 Cut each red mullet in half, then add the pieces to the pan, pushing them into the sauce. Simmer gently for a further 5–6 minutes, or until the fish is just cooked.

4 Carefully stir in the olives, the preserved lemon and the chopped coriander. Season to taste and serve with couscous.

COOK'S TIP

If preserved lemons are not available, add the grated rind of 1 lemon and 1 tablespoon lemon juice.

Hake Steaks with Chermoula

The cooking time may seem long and indeed you could decrease it slightly if you prefer, but in Morocco they like their fish well cooked.

NUTRITIONAL INFORMATION

Calories 590	Sugars 1g	
Protein 42g	Fat 46g	
Carbohydrate . . . 2g	Saturates 7g	

🍲

5 mins, plus
1 hr marinating ⏲ 40 mins

SERVES 4

I N G R E D I E N T S

4 hake steaks, about 225 g/8 oz each

115 g/4 oz pitted green olives

MARINADE

6 tbsp finely chopped fresh coriander

6 tbsp finely chopped fresh parsley

6 garlic cloves, crushed

1 tbsp ground cumin

1 tsp ground coriander

1 tbsp paprika

pinch cayenne pepper

150 ml/5 fl oz fresh lemon juice

300 ml/10 fl oz cups olive oil

1 Mix together the marinade ingredients. Wash and dry the hake steaks and place in an ovenproof dish. Pour the marinade over the fish and leave for at least 1 hour and preferably overnight.

2 Before cooking, scatter the olives over the fish. Cover the dish with foil.

3 Cook in a preheated oven at 160°C/ 325°F/Gas Mark 3. Cook for 35–40 minutes, or until the fish is tender. Serve with freshly cooked vegetables.

VARIATION

Remove the fish from the marinade and dust with seasoned flour. Fry in oil or clarified butter until golden. Warm through the marinade, but do not boil, and serve as a sauce with lemon slices.

Sea Bass with Artichokes

Baby artichokes are slowly cooked with olive oil, garlic, thyme and lemon to create a soft blend of flavours that harmonizes very well with the fish.

NUTRITIONAL INFORMATION

Calories	 400	Sugars	.... 3g
Protein	.... 28g	Fat	.... 30g
Carbohydrate	... 7g	Saturates	...... 5g

30 mins   30 mins

SERVES 6

INGREDIENTS

1.8 kg/4 lb baby artichokes

2½ tbsp fresh lemon juice, plus the cut halves of the lemon

150 ml/5 fl oz olive oil

10 garlic cloves, finely sliced

1 tbsp fresh thyme plus extra, to garnish

6 x 115 g/4 oz sea bass fillets

1 tbsp olive oil

salt and pepper

crusty bread, to serve

1 Peel away the tough outer leaves of each artichoke until the yellow-green heart is revealed. Slice off the pointed top at about halfway between the point and the top of the stem. Cut off the stem and pare off what is left of the dark green leaves surrounding the base.

2 Submerge the prepared artichokes in water containing the cut halves of the lemon to prevent them browning. When all the artichokes have been prepared, turn them, choke side down, and slice thinly.

3 Warm the olive oil in a large saucepan and add the sliced artichokes, garlic, thyme, lemon juice and seasoning. Cover and cook over a low heat for 20–30 minutes, without colouring, until tender.

4 Meanwhile, brush the sea bass fillets with the remaining olive oil and season well. Cook on a preheated ridged grill pan or barbecue for 3–4 minutes on each side, or until just tender.

5 Divide the stewed artichokes between serving plates and top each with a sea bass fillet. Garnish with chopped thyme and serve with lots of crusty bread.

VARIATION

Artichokes cooked this way also suit cod, halibut or salmon.

Sea Bass with Ratatouille

Sea bass, surely the king of round fish, is served with a highly flavoured sauce of ratatouille, and a basil dressing.

NUTRITIONAL INFORMATION

Calories 373	Sugars 9g
Protein 42g	Fat 18g
Carbohydrate ..10g	Saturates 3g

15 mins, plus 30 mins standing ⏱ 1 hr

SERVES 4

I N G R E D I E N T S

2 large sea bass, filleted

olive oil, for brushing

salt and pepper

R A T A T O U I L L E

1 medium onion

½ red pepper, deseeded

½ green pepper, deseeded

1 large aubergine

2 medium courgettes

1 tbsp sea salt

4 tbsp olive oil

2 garlic cloves, crushed

2 large ripe tomatoes, skinned and chopped

1 tbsp freshly chopped basil

D R E S S I N G

5 tbsp roughly chopped fresh basil

2 garlic cloves, roughly chopped

4 tbsp olive oil

1 tbsp lemon juice

salt and pepper

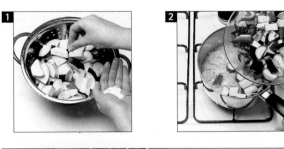

1 To make the ratatouille, cut the onion, red and green peppers, aubergine and courgettes into bite-sized chunks. Put the aubergine and courgettes in a colander, sprinkle with the salt and set aside to drain for 30 minutes. Rinse the salted vegetables and pat dry on kitchen paper. Set aside.

2 Heat the oil in a large saucepan and add the onion and garlic. Cook gently for 10 minutes, or until softened. Add the peppers, aubergine and courgette. Season to taste with salt and pepper and stir well. Cover and cook very gently for 30 minutes, or until all the vegetables have softened, stirring occasionally. Add the chopped tomatoes and continue cooking for a further 15 minutes.

3 Meanwhile make the dressing. Put the basil, garlic and half the olive oil into a food processor and blend until finely chopped. Add the remaining olive oil, lemon juice and seasoning.

4 Season the sea bass fillets and brush with a little oil. Preheat a frying pan until very hot and add the fish, skin side down. Cook for 2–3 minutes, or until the skin is browned and crispy. Turn the fish and cook for a further 2–3 minutes, or until it is just cooked through.

5 To serve, stir the basil into the ratatouille, then divide it between 4 serving plates. Top with the fried fish and spoon around the dressing.

Tuna with Flavoured Butter

Meaty tuna steaks have enough flavour to stand up to the robust taste of anchovies. Serve this with pan-fried potatoes or a mixed rice dish.

NUTRITIONAL INFORMATION

Calories	 564	Sugars	. . . . 0g
Protein	. . . . . . 5.5g	Fat	. . . . 38g
Carbohydrate	. . . 0g	Saturates	. . . . . 19g

15 mins, plus 15 mins chilling

20 mins

SERVES 4

INGREDIENTS

olive oil

4 thick tuna steaks, each about 225 g/8 oz and 2 cm/¾ inch thick

ANCHOVY AND ORANGE BUTTER

8 anchovy fillets in oil, drained

4 spring onions, finely chopped

1 tbsp finely grated orange rind

115 g/4 oz unsalted butter, softened

¼ tsp lemon juice

pepper

TO GARNISH

fresh flat-leaved parsley sprigs

orange rind strips

1 To make the anchovy and orange butter, very finely chop the anchovies and put them in a bowl with the spring onions, orange rind and softened butter. Beat until all the ingredients are blended together, seasoning with lemon juice and pepper to taste.

2 Place the flavoured butter on a sheet of baking paper and roll up into a log shape. Fold over the ends and place the roll in the freezer for about 15 minutes, or until it becomes firm.

3 To cook the tuna, heat a ridged frying pan over a high heat. Lightly brush the pan with olive oil, add the tuna steaks and fry for 2 minutes. Turn the steaks over and fry for 2 minutes for rare, or up to 4 minutes for well done. Season to taste with salt and pepper.

4 Transfer to a warm plate and put 2 thin slices of anchovy butter on each tuna steak. Garnish with parsley sprigs and orange rind and serve at once, while the tuna is still hot.

VARIATION

If you particularly like hot, spicy food, add a pinch of dried chilli flakes to the butter mixture.

Swordfish à la Maltese

The firm texture of swordfish means it is often simply grilled, but it also lends itself to this delicate technique of cooking in a paper parcel.

NUTRITIONAL INFORMATION

Calories	303	Sugars	10g
Protein	34g	Fat	13g
Carbohydrate	13g	Saturates	3g

🍲 🍲

🥘 15 mins   🕐 25 mins

MAKES 4

INGREDIENTS

1 tbsp fennel seeds

2 tbsp fruity extra-virgin olive oil, plus extra for brushing and drizzling

2 large onions, thinly sliced

1 small garlic clove, crushed

4 swordfish steaks, about 175 g/6 oz each

1 large lemon, cut in half

2 large sun-ripened tomatoes, finely chopped

4 sprigs fresh thyme

salt and pepper

1 Place the fennel seeds in a dry frying pan over a medium-high heat and toast, stirring, until they give off their aroma, watching carefully that they do not burn. Immediately tip out of the pan on to a plate. Set aside.

2 Heat the the 2 tablespoons of olive oil in the pan. Add the onions and fry for 5 minutes, stirring occasionally. Add the garlic and continue frying until the onions are very soft and tender, but not brown. Remove the pan from the heat.

3 Cut out four 30 cm/12 inch circles of baking paper. Very lightly brush the centre of each paper circle with olive oil. Equally divide the onions between the paper circles, flattening them out to about the size of the fish steaks.

4 Top the onions in each parcel with a swordfish steak. Squeeze lemon juice over the fish steaks and drizzle with a little olive oil. Scatter with the tomatoes and fennel seeds, add a sprig of thyme to each and season with salt and pepper to taste.

5 Fold the edges of the paper together tightly so that no juices escape during cooking. Place the parcels on a baking sheet and cook in a preheated oven at 200°C/400°F/ Gas Mark 6 for 20 minutes.

6 To test if the fish is cooked, open one parcel and pierce the flesh with a knife. If cooked it should flake easily. Serve straight from the paper parcels.

Red Mullet with Fennel

Fresh thyme, which grows wild throughout the Mediterranean, flavours this rustic dish, in which the fish is wrapped in vine leaves.

NUTRITIONAL INFORMATION

Calories	320	Sugars	8g
Protein	37g	Fat	16g
Carbohydrate	9g	Saturates	1g

🍳 🍳

25 mins   35 mins

SERVES 4

I N G R E D I E N T S

3 tbsp olive oil, plus extra for rubbing

2 large red peppers, cored, deseeded and thinly sliced

2 large bulbs fennel, trimmed and thinly sliced

1 large clove garlic, crushed

8 sprigs fresh thyme, plus extra for garnishing

20–24 vine leaves in brine

1 lemon

4 red mullet, about 225 g/8 oz each, scaled and gutted

salt and pepper

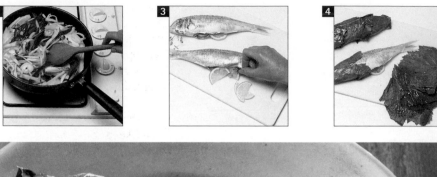

1 Heat the oil in a large frying pan over a medium–low heat. Add the peppers, fennel, garlic and 4 sprigs of thyme and stir together. Cook, stirring occasionally, for about 20 minutes, or until the vegetables are cooked thoroughly and are very soft, but not browned.

2 Meanwhile, rinse the vine leaves under cold, running water and pat dry with kitchen paper. Slice 4 thin slices off the lemon, then cut each slice in half. Finely grate the rind of ½ the lemon.

3 Stuff the mullet cavities with the lemon slices and remaining thyme sprigs. Rub a little olive oil on each fish and sprinkle with the lemon rind. Season with salt and pepper to taste.

4 Depending on the size of the mullet and the vine leaves, wrap 5 or 6 vine leaves around each mullet, to completely enclose. Put the wrapped mullet on top of the fennel and peppers. Cover the pan and cook over a medium–low heat for 12–15 minutes, or until the fish are

cooked through and the flesh flakes easily when tested with the tip of a knife.

5 Transfer the cooked fish to individual plates and spoon the fennel and peppers alongside. Garnish with thyme sprigs and serve.

Scallops with Champagne

Coming straight from the finest Riviera restaurants, this rich and extravagant dish is surprisingly simple.

NUTRITIONAL INFORMATION

Calories	 504	Sugars	.... 3g
Protein	 10	Fat	.... 49g
Carbohydrate	... 4g	Saturates	..... 31g

🍲 20 mins   🕐 5 mins

SERVES 4

INGREDIENTS

generous pinch of saffron threads

60 g/2¼ oz unsalted butter

20 large scallops with the corals, each at least 2.5 cm/1 inch thick, shelled with any juices reserved

4 tbsp dry champagne or sparkling wine

300 ml/10 fl oz double heavy cream

½ lemon

salt and pepper

fresh flat-leaved parsley sprigs, to garnish

1 Heat a large dry frying pan, preferably non-stick, over a high heat. Add the saffron threads and toast just until they start to give off their aroma. Immediately tip on to a plate and set aside.

2 Melt half the butter in the pan. Add half the scallops and fry for 2 minutes. Turn and fry for a further 1½–2 minutes, or until the scallops are set and the flesh is opaque all the way though when you pierce one with a knife (see Cook's Tip).

3 Transfer the scallops to a hot dish, cover and keep warm while cooking the rest in the same way, adding more butter to the pan as necessary.

4 Add the saffron to the cooking juices and pour in the champagne, cream and any reserved scallop juices, stirring. Bring to the boil, then lower the heat slightly and bubble for about 10 minutes, or until the sauce is reduced to a consistency that coats the back of a spoon.

5 Add freshly squeezed lemon juice and salt and pepper to taste. Return the scallops to the pan and stir until just heated through. Transfer to 4 plates and garnish with parsley. Serve at once.

COOK'S TIP

The exact cooking time depends on the thickness of the scallops. If the scallops are thinner, cook them for only 1½ minutes on each side. Take great care not to overcook them.

Pasta with Broccoli & Cheese

Orecchiette, the cup-shape pasta from southern Italy, is excellent for this filling dish because it scoops up the robust, chunky sauce.

NUTRITIONAL INFORMATION

Calories 685	Sugars 4g
Protein 33g	Fat 29g
Carbohydrate .. 78g	Saturates 9g

🥟 🥟

🍲 15 mins   🕐 25 mins

SERVES 4

INGREDIENTS

500 g/1 lb 2 oz broccoli

400 g/14 oz dried orecchiette

5 tbsp olive oil

2 large garlic cloves, crushed

50 g/1¾ oz canned anchovy fillets in oil, drained and finely chopped

60 g/2¼ oz Parmesan cheese

60 g/2¼ oz pecorino cheese

salt and pepper

1 Bring 2 pans of lightly salted water to the boil. Chop the broccoli florets and stems into small, bite-sized pieces. Add the broccoli to one pan and cook until very tender. Drain and set aside.

2 Put the pasta in the other pan and cook for 10–12 minutes, or until al dente, or firm to the bite.

3 Meanwhile, heat the olive oil in a large pan over a medium heat. Add the garlic and fry for 3 minutes, stirring, without allowing it to brown. Add the chopped anchovies to the oil and cook for 3 minutes, stirring and mashing with a wooden spoon to break them up. Meanwhile, finely grate the cheeses.

4 Drain the pasta, add to the pan of anchovies and stir. Add the broccoli and stir to mix.

5 Add the grated Parmesan and pecorino to the pasta and stir constantly over medium–high heat until the cheeses melt and the pasta and broccoli are coated.

6 Adjust the seasoning to taste – the anchovies and cheeses are salty, so you will need only to add pepper, if anything. Spoon the pasta into bowls or on to plates and serve at once.

VARIATIONS
Add dried chilli flakes to taste with the garlic in Step 3, if you want. If you have difficulty in finding orecchiette, try using pasta bows instead.

Pasta with Tuna & Lemon

Corkscrew-shaped fusilli and thin pasta carareccia are the best pasta shapes for this recipe because the creamy sauce is caught in the twists.

NUTRITIONAL INFORMATION

Calories	891	Sugars	6g
Protein	27g	Fat	55g
Carbohydrate	77g	Saturates	31g

10 mins   20 mins

SERVES 4

INGREDIENTS

400 g/14 oz dried fusilli

60 g/2¼ oz butter, diced

300 ml/10 fl oz double cream

4 tbsp lemon juice

1 tbsp grated lemon rind

½ tsp anchovy essence

200 g/7 oz canned tuna in olive oil, drained and flaked

salt and pepper

TO GARNISH

2 tbsp finely chopped fresh parsley

grated lemon rind

1 Bring a large saucepan of lightly salted water to the boil. Cook the pasta for 10–12 minutes, or according to the instructions on the packet until just al dente (tender but firm to the bite). Drain.

2 Meanwhile, make the sauce. Melt the butter in a large frying pan. Stir in the double cream and lemon juice and leave to simmer, stirring, for about 2 minutes, or until slightly thickened. Stir in the lemon rind and anchovy essence.

3 Drain the pasta well. Add the pasta sauce and toss until well coated. Add the tuna and gently toss until well blended but not too broken up.

4 Season to taste with salt and pepper. Transfer to a serving platter and garnish with the parsley and lemon rind. Grind over some pepper and serve at once.

Pasta & Anchovy Sauce

This is an ideal dish for cooks in a hurry, as it is prepared in minutes from storecupboard ingredients.

NUTRITIONAL INFORMATION

Calories 712	Sugars 4g
Protein 25g	Fat 34g
Carbohydrate . . 81g	Saturates 8g

10 mins   20 mins

SERVES 4

INGREDIENTS

90 ml/3¼ fl oz olive oil

2 garlic cloves, crushed

60 g/2¼ oz canned anchovy fillets, drained

450 g/1 lb dried spaghetti

60 g/2¼ oz pesto (see page 21)

2 tbsp finely chopped fresh oregano

85 g/3 oz grated Parmesan cheese, plus
    extra for serving

salt and pepper

2 fresh oregano sprigs, to garnish

1 Reserving 1 tablespoon, heat the oil in a small saucepan. Add the garlic and fry for 3 minutes.

2 Lower the heat, stir in the anchovies and cook, stirring occasionally, until the anchovies have disintegrated.

3 Bring a large saucepan of lightly salted water to the boil. Add the spaghetti and the reserved olive oil and cook for 8–10 minutes, or according to the instructions on the packet, until just tender, but still firm to the bite.

4 Add the pesto and chopped fresh oregano to the anchovy mixture, then season with pepper to taste.

5 Drain the spaghetti, using a slotted spoon, and transfer to a warm serving dish. Pour the pesto and anchovy mixture over the spaghetti and then sprinkle over the grated Parmesan cheese.

6 Garnish with oregano sprigs and serve with extra cheese.

COOK'S TIP

If you find canned anchovies rather too salty, soak them in a saucer of cold milk for 5 minutes, drain and pat dry with kitchen paper before using. The milk absorbs the salt.

Italian Cod

This simple Italian dish of cod roasted with a mixed herb, lemon and walnut crust is a delicious main course.

NUTRITIONAL INFORMATION

Calories	313	Sugars	0.4g
Protein	29g	Fat	20g
Carbohydrate	6g	Saturates	5g

🐾 🐾

10 mins   ⏲ 35 mins

SERVES 4

INGREDIENTS

25 g/1 oz butter

50 g/1¾ oz wholemeal breadcrumbs

25 g/1 oz chopped walnuts

grated rind and juice of 2 lemons

2 sprigs rosemary, stalks removed

2 tbsp chopped parsley

4 cod fillets, each about 150 g/5½ oz

1 garlic clove, crushed

3 tbsp walnut oil

1 small red chilli, diced

salad leaves, to serve

1 Melt the butter in a large saucepan, stirring. Remove the pan from the heat. Add the breadcrumbs, walnuts, the rind and juice of 1 lemon, half the rosemary and half the parsley to the butter.

2 Press the breadcrumb mixture over the top of the cod fillets. Place the cod fillets in a shallow, foil-lined roasting tin.

3 Bake the cod fillets in a preheated oven at 200°C/400°F/Gas Mark 6 for 25–30 minutes, or until they are just cooked. Take care not to overcook.

4 Mix the garlic, the remaining lemon rind and juice, rosemary, parsley and chilli in a bowl. Beat in the walnut oil and mix to combine. Drizzle the dressing over the cod steaks as soon as they are cooked.

5 Transfer the cod fillets to serving plates and serve immediately.

VARIATION

If preferred, the walnuts may be omitted from the crust. In addition, extra-virgin olive oil can be used instead of walnut oil, if you prefer.

Rich Lobster Risotto

Although lobster is expensive, this dish is worth it. Keeping it simple allows the lobster flavour to come through.

NUTRITIONAL INFORMATION

Calories	688	Sugars	3g
Protein	32g	Fat	31g
Carbohydrate	69g	Saturates	16g

10 mins   40 mins

SERVES 4

INGREDIENTS

1 tbsp vegetable oil

60 g/2¼ oz unsalted butter

2 shallots, finely chopped

300 g/10½ oz arborio or carnaroli rice

½ tsp cayenne pepper, or to taste

80 ml/3 fl oz dry white vermouth

1.5 litres/2¾ pints shellfish, fish or light chicken stock, simmering

225 g/8 oz cherry tomatoes, halved and deseeded

2–3 tbsp double or whipping cream

450 g/1 lb cooked lobster meat, cut into coarse chunks

2 tbsp chopped fresh chervil or dill

salt and white pepper

1 Heat the oil and half the butter in a large heavy-based saucepan over a medium heat. Add the shallots and cook for about 2 minutes, or until just beginning to soften. Add the rice and cayenne pepper and cook, stirring frequently, for about 2 minutes, or until the rice is translucent and well coated with the oil and butter.

2 Pour in the vermouth; it will bubble and steam rapidly and evaporate almost immediately. Add a ladleful (about 225 ml/8 fl oz) of the simmering stock and cook, stirring, until the stock is absorbed.

3 Continue adding the stock, about half a ladleful at a time, allowing each addition to be absorbed before adding the next, taking care never to allow the rice to cook dry. This should take 20–25 minutes.

The risotto should have a creamy consistency and the rice should be tender, but firm to the bite.

4 Stir in the tomatoes and cream and cook for about 2 minutes.

5 Add the cooked lobster meat, with the remaining butter and chervil, and cook long enough to just heat the lobster meat gently. Serve immediately.

Tuna Niçoise Salad

This is a version of the classic French *salade niçoise*. It is a substantial salad, suitable for a lunch or a light summer supper.

NUTRITIONAL INFORMATION

Calories 109	Sugars 1.1g	
Protein 7.2g	Fat 7.0g	
Carbohydrate .. 4.8g	Saturates 1.2g	

10 mins   20 mins

SERVES 4

INGREDIENTS

4 eggs

450 g/1 lb new potatoes

115 g/4 oz dwarf green beans, trimmed and halved

2 x 175 g/6 oz tuna steaks

6 tbsp olive oil, plus extra for brushing

1 garlic clove, crushed

1½ tsp Dijon mustard

2 tsp lemon juice

2 tbsp chopped fresh basil

2 little gem lettuces

200 g/7 oz cherry tomatoes, halved

175 g/6 oz cucumber, peeled, halved lengthways and sliced

50 g/1¾ oz stoned black olives

50 g/1¾ oz canned anchovies in oil, drained

salt and pepper

2 Cook the potatoes in boiling salted water for 10–12 minutes, or until tender. Add the green beans 3 minutes before the end of the cooking time. Drain both vegetables well and refresh under cold water. Drain well.

3 Wash and dry the tuna steaks. Brush with a little olive oil and season. Cook on a preheated ridged grill pan for 2–3 minutes each side, until just tender but still slightly pink in the centre. Set aside to rest.

4 For the dressing, whisk together the garlic, mustard, lemon juice, basil and seasoning. Whisk in the olive oil.

5 To assemble the salad, break apart the lettuces and tear into large pieces. Divide between individual serving plates. Add the potatoes and beans, tomatoes, cucumber and olives. Toss lightly together. Shell the eggs and cut into quarters lengthways. Arrange these on top of the salad. Scatter over the anchovies.

6 Flake the tuna steaks and arrange on the salad. Pour over the dressing and serve immediately.

1 Bring a small saucepan of water to the boil. Add the eggs and cook for 7–9 minutes from when the water returns to a boil – 7 minutes for a slightly soft centre, or 9 minutes for a firm centre. Drain and refresh under cold running water. Set the pan aside.

Baked Goat's Cheese Salad

Scrumptious hot goat's cheese and herb croûtes are served with a tossed leafy salad to make an excellent light snack, capturing Provençal flavours.

NUTRITIONAL INFORMATION

Calories 509	Sugars 3g	
Protein 18g	Fat 33g	
Carbohydrate .. 35g	Saturates 10g	

15 mins   10 mins

SERVES 4

INGREDIENTS

250 g/9 oz mixed salad leaves, such as rocket, lamb's lettuce and chicory

12 slices French bread

extra-virgin olive oil, for brushing

12 thin slices of Provençal goat's cheese, such as Picodon

fresh herbs, such as rosemary, thyme or oregano, finely chopped

extra French bread, to serve

DRESSING

6 tbsp extra-virgin olive oil

3 tbsp red wine vinegar

½ tsp sugar

½ tsp Dijon mustard

salt and pepper

1 To prepare the salad, rinse the leaves under cold water and pat dry with a tea towel. Wrap in kitchen paper and put in a plastic bag. Seal tightly and chill until required.

2 To make the dressing, place all the ingredients in a screw-top jar and shake until well blended. Season with salt and pepper to taste and shake again. Set aside while preparing the croûtes.

3 Toast the slices of bread on both sides until they are crisp. Brush a little olive oil on one side of each slice while still hot, so the oil is absorbed.

4 Place the croûtes on a baking sheet and top each with a slice of cheese. Sprinkle the herbs over the cheese and drizzle with olive oil. Bake in a preheated oven at 180°C/350°F/Gas Mark 4 for 5 minutes.

5 While the croûtes are in the oven, place the salad leaves in a bowl. Shake the dressing again, pour it over the leaves and toss together. Divide the salad between 4 plates.

6 Transfer the hot croûtes to the salads. Serve at once with extra slices of French bread.

Lobster Salad

Lobsters are as expensive along the Mediterranean as they are in other parts of the world, so it is best to prepare them simply.

NUTRITIONAL INFORMATION

Calories	487	Sugars	2g
Protein	24g	Fat	42g
Carbohydrate	2g	Saturates	6g

15 mins   6 mins

SERVES 2

INGREDIENTS

2 raw lobster tails

salt and pepper

LEMON-DILL MAYONNAISE

1 large lemon

1 large egg yolk

½ tsp Dijon mustard

150 ml/5 fl oz olive oil

1 tbsp chopped fresh dill

TO GARNISH

radicchio leaves

lemon wedges

fresh dill sprigs

1 To make the lemon-dill mayonnaise, finely grate the rind from the lemon and squeeze the juice. Beat the egg yolk in a small bowl and beat in the mustard and 1 teaspoon of the lemon juice.

2 Using a balloon whisk or electric mixer, beat in the olive oil, drop by drop, until a thick mayonnaise forms. Stir in half the lemon rind and 1 tablespoon of the juice.

3 Season with salt and pepper, and add more lemon juice if desired. Stir in the dill and cover with cling film. Chill the mayonnaise until required.

4 Bring a large saucepan of salted water to the boil. Add the lobster tails and cook for 6 minutes, or until the flesh is opaque and the shells are red. Drain immediately and leave to cool completely.

5 Remove the lobster flesh from the shells and cut into bite-sized pieces. Arrange the radicchio leaves on individual plates and top with the lobster flesh. Place a spoonful of the lemon-dill mayonnaise on the side. Garnish with lemon wedges and dill sprigs and serve.

Ratatouille

A slow-cooked Provençal vegetable stew, this goes particularly well with roast lamb, but it is also excellent with any grilled meat or poultry.

NUTRITIONAL INFORMATION

Calories ...... 157 Sugars 11g
Protein .... 4g Fat 9g
Carbohydrate .. 14g Saturates 1g

🐾 🐾

🥘 10 mins, plus
30 mins draining

🕐 55 mins

SERVES 4–6

INGREDIENTS

1 large aubergine, about 300 g/10½ oz

5 tbsp olive oil

2 large onions, thinly sliced

2 large garlic cloves, crushed

4 courgettes, sliced

800 g/28 oz canned chopped tomatoes

1 tsp sugar

1 bouquet garni of 2 sprigs fresh thyme,
  2 large sprigs parsley, 1 sprig basil and
  1 bay leaf, tied in a 7.5 cm/3 inch piece
  of celery

salt and pepper

fresh basil leaves, to garnish

1 Coarsely chop the aubergine, then place in a colander. Sprinkle with salt and leave for 30 minutes to drain. Rinse well and pat dry.

2 Heat the oil in a large heavy-based flameproof casserole over a medium heat. Add the thinly sliced onions, lower the heat and fry, stirring frequently, for 10 minutes.

3 Add the garlic and continue to fry for 2 minutes, stirring until the onions are very tender, and lightly browned.

4 Add the aubergine, courgettes, tomatoes and their juice, the sugar, bouquet garni and salt and pepper to taste. Bring to the boil, then lower the heat to very low, cover and leave for 30 minutes.

5 Adjust the seasoning. Remove and discard the bouquet garni. Garnish the vegetable stew with basil leaves and serve.

COOK'S TIP

This is equally good served hot, at room temperature or chilled. To make a vegetarian meal, serve it over cooked couscous.

Glazed Baby Onions

These onions are bathed in a rich, intensely flavoured glaze, making them a good accompaniment to any grilled or roasted meat.

NUTRITIONAL INFORMATION

Calories 81   Sugars 8g
Protein . . . . 1g   Fat 4g
Carbohydrate . . . 11g   Saturates 1g

10 mins   25 mins

SERVES 4–6

I N G R E D I E N T S

500 g/1 lb 2 oz baby onions

2 tbsp olive oil

2 large garlic cloves, crushed

300 ml/10 fl oz vegetable or chicken stock

1 tbsp fresh thyme leaves

1 tbsp light brown sugar

2 tbsp red wine vinegar

about ½ tbsp best-quality balsamic vinegar

salt and pepper

fresh thyme sprigs, to garnish

1 Bring water to the boil. Put the onions in a heatproof bowl, cover with boiling water, and leave to stand for 2 minutes. Drain well and allow to cool.

2 Using a small knife and your fingers, peel off the skins, which should now slip off quite easily.

3 Heat the olive oil in a large frying pan over a medium–high heat. Add the peeled onions and cook, stirring, for about 8 minutes, or until they are golden on all sides.

4 Add the garlic and cook for 2 minutes, stirring. Add the stock, thyme leaves, sugar and red wine vinegar, stirring until the sugar has dissolved.

5 Bring to the boil, then lower the heat and simmer for 10 minutes, or until the onions are tender when you pierce them with the tip of a knife and the cooking liquid is reduced to a syrupy glaze.

6 Season to taste with salt and pepper and balsamic vinegar. Transfer to a serving dish and serve hot or cold, garnished with fresh thyme sprigs.

Mozzarella & Tomato Salad

Take advantage of the delicious varieties of cherry tomato which are available to make a refreshing, eye-catching Italian-style salad.

NUTRITIONAL INFORMATION

Calories 295   Sugars 3g
Protein .... 9g   Fat 27g
Carbohydrate ... 3g   Saturates 7g

🥪 10 mins, plus 4 hrs chilling   🕐 0 mins

SERVES 4–6

I N G R E D I E N T S

450 g/1 lb cherry tomatoes

4 spring onions

125 ml/4 fl oz extra-virgin olive oil

2 tbsp best-quality balsamic vinegar

200 g/7 oz buffalo mozzarella (see Cook's Tip), cut into cubes

15 g/½ oz fresh flat-leaved parsley

25 g/1 oz fresh basil leaves

salt and pepper

1 Using a sharp knife, cut the tomatoes in half and put in a large bowl. Trim the spring onions and chop the green and white parts finely, then add to the bowl.

2 Pour in the olive oil and the balsamic vinegar and toss the salad using your hands. Season with salt and pepper to taste, add the mozzarella cubes, and toss again. Cover the dish with clingfilm and chill for 4 hours.

3 Remove the salad from the refrigerator 10 minutes before serving. Chop the parsley finely and add to the salad. Tear the basil leaves over the salad and toss all the ingredients once more, then adjust the seasoning to taste and serve.

COOK'S TIP

For the best flavour, buy buffalo mozzarella – mozzarella di bufala – rather than the factory-made cow's milk version. This salad would also look good made with bocconcini, which are small balls of mozzarella. Look out for these in Italian delicatessens.

Green Tabbouleh

Tomatoes are sometimes included in this refreshing bulgar wheat salad from Turkey, but this version features green herbs and vegetables.

NUTRITIONAL INFORMATION

Calories 333	Sugars 4g
Protein 9g	Fat 24g
Carbohydrate . . 59g	Saturates 8g

🍲 🍲

10 mins, plus
10 mins standing

⏱ 0 mins

SERVES 4

I N G R E D I E N T S

300 g/10½ oz bulgar wheat

200 g/7 oz cucumber

6 spring onions

15 g/½ oz fresh flat-leaved parsley

1 unwaxed lemon

about 2 tbsp garlic-flavoured olive oil

salt and pepper

1 Bring a kettle of water to the boil. Place the bulgar wheat in a heatproof bowl, pour over 600 ml/1 pint boiling water and cover with an upturned plate. Set aside for at least 20 minutes, or until the wheat absorbs the water and becomes tender.

2 While the wheat is soaking, cut the cucumber in half lengthways and then cut each half into 3 strips lengthways. Using a teaspoon, scoop out and discard the seeds. Chop the cucumber strips into small pieces. Put the cucumber pieces in a serving bowl.

3 Trim away the top of the green parts of each of the spring onions, then cut each in half lengthways. Chop finely and add to the cucumber.

4 Place the parsley on a chopping board and sprinkle with salt. Using a cook's knife, chop the leaves and stems very finely.

Add to the bowl with the cucumber and spring onions. Grate the lemon rind finely into the bowl.

5 When the bulgar wheat is cool enough to handle, either squeeze out any excess water with your hands or press out the water through a sieve, then add to the bowl with the other ingredients.

6 Cut the lemon in half and squeeze the juice of one half over the salad. Add 2 tablespoons of the garlic-flavoured oil and stir all the ingredients together. Season to taste and add extra lemon juice or oil if needed. Cover and chill until required.

COOK'S TIP
Serve as part of a meze with dips such as Hummus (see page 11).

Broad Beans with Feta

This simple dish captures the heady flavours of the Greek islands, and makes a good hot or cold vegetable accompaniment to a main meal.

NUTRITIONAL INFORMATION

Calories	140	Sugars	1g
Protein	6g	Fat	10g
Carbohydrate	6g	Saturates	3g

10 mins   2 mins

SERVES 4–6

INGREDIENTS

500 g/1 lb 2 oz shelled broad beans

4 tbsp extra-virgin olive oil

1 tbsp lemon juice

1 tbsp finely chopped fresh dill, plus a little extra for garnishing

60 g/2¼ oz feta cheese, drained and diced

salt and pepper

lemon wedges, to serve

1 Bring a saucepan of water to the boil. Add the broad beans and cook for about 2 minutes, or until tender. Drain well.

2 When the beans are cool enough to handle, remove and discard the outer skins, to reveal the bright green beans underneath. (See Cook's Tip.) Put the peeled beans in a serving bowl.

3 Whisk together the olive oil and lemon juice, then season with salt and pepper to taste. Pour over the warm beans, add the dill and stir together.

4 If serving hot, toss with the feta cheese and sprinkle with extra dill.

Alternatively, leave to cool and chill until required. Remove from the refrigerator 10 minutes before serving, season, then sprinkle with the feta and extra dill. Serve with lemon wedges.

COOK'S TIP

If you are lucky enough to have very young broad beans at the start of the season, it isn't necessary to remove the outer skins.

Panzanella

This traditional, refreshing Italian salad of day-old bread is ideal to serve for lunch or as a simple supper on a hot day.

NUTRITIONAL INFORMATION

Calories 213	Sugars 11g	
Protein 7g	Fat 6g	
Carbohydrate .. 33g	Saturates 1g	

🥪 🥪

🍲 15 mins, plus 50 mins standing   ⏱ 10 mins

SERVES 4–6

I N G R E D I E N T S

250 g/9 oz herb foccacia ciabatta or French bread

4 large, vine-ripened tomatoes

extra-virgin olive oil

4 red, yellow and/or orange peppers

100 g/3½ oz cucumber

1 large red onion, finely chopped

8 canned anchovy fillets, drained and chopped

2 tbsp capers in brine, rinsed and patted dry

about 4 tbsp red wine vinegar

about 2 tbsp best-quality balsamic vinegar

salt and pepper

fresh basil leaves, to garnish

1 Cut the bread into 2.5 cm/1 inch cubes and place in a large bowl. Working over a plate to catch any juices, quarter the tomatoes; reserve the juices. Using a teaspoon, scoop out the cores and seeds, then finely chop the flesh. Add the flesh to the bread cubes.

2 Drizzle 5 tablespoons of olive oil over the mixture and toss with your hands until well coated. Pour in the reserved tomato juice and toss again. Set aside for about 30 minutes.

3 Meanwhile, cut the peppers in half and remove the cores and seeds. Place on a grill rack under a preheated hot grill and grill for 10 minutes, or until the skins are charred and the flesh softened. Place in a plastic bag, seal and then set aside for 20 minutes to allow the steam to loosen the skins. Remove the skins, then chop finely.

4 Cut the cucumber in half lengthways, then cut each half into 3 strips lengthways. Using a teaspoon, scoop out and discard the seeds. Dice the cucumber.

5 Add the onion, peppers, cucumber, anchovy fillets and capers to the bread and toss together. Sprinkle with the red wine and balsamic vinegars and season to taste with salt and pepper. Drizzle with extra olive oil or vinegar if necessary, but be cautious that it does not become too greasy or soggy. Sprinkle the fresh basil leaves over the salad and serve at once.

Potato & Sausage Salad

Sliced Italian sausage blends well with the other Mediterranean flavours of sun-dried tomato and basil in this salad.

NUTRITIONAL INFORMATION

Calories	 450	Sugars	. . . . 6g
Protein	. . . . 13g	Fat	. . . . 28g
Carbohydrate	. . 38g	Saturates	. . . . . . 1g

15 mins   20 mins

SERVES 4

INGREDIENTS

450 g/1 lb waxy potatoes

1 raddichio or lollo rosso lettuce

1 green pepper, sliced

175 g/6 oz Italian sausage, sliced

1 red onion, halved and sliced

125 g/4½ oz sun-dried tomatoes, sliced

2 tbsp shredded fresh basil

DRESSING

1 tbsp balsamic vinegar

1 tsp tomato purée

2 tbsp olive oil

salt and pepper

1 Cook the potatoes in a saucepan of boiling water for 20 minutes, or until cooked through. Drain and leave to cool.

COOK'S TIP

Any sliced Italian sausage or salami can be used in this salad. Italy is home of the salami and there are numerous varieties to choose from – those from the south tend to be more highly spiced than those from the north of the country.

2 Line a large serving platter with the radicchio or lollo rosso lettuce leaves.

3 Slice the cooled potatoes and arrange them in layers on the lettuce-lined serving platter together with the sliced green pepper, sliced Italian sausage, red onion slices, sun-dried tomatoes and shredded fresh basil.

4 In a small bowl, whisk the balsamic vinegar, tomato purée and olive oil together and season to taste with salt and pepper. Pour the dressing over the potato salad and serve immediately.

Figs with Orange Blossom

Luscious, sweet fresh figs are piled high on market stalls throughout the Mediterranean during the summer.

NUTRITIONAL INFORMATION

Calories ...... 220 Sugars 13g
Protein .... 3g Fat 18g
Carbohydrate .. 14g Saturates 9g

🔥 🔥

🍽 10 mins   🕐 0 mins

SERVES 4

I N G R E D I E N T S

8 large fresh figs

4 large fresh fig leaves, if available, rinsed and dried

ORANGE-BLOSSOM CREAM

125 ml/4 fl oz crème fraîche, homemade (see below) or bought

4 tbsp orange-blossom water

1 tsp orange-blossom honey

finely grated rind of ½ orange

2 tbsp flaked almonds, to decorate (optional)

HOMEMADE CREME FRAICHE (OPTIONAL)

2 tbsp buttermilk

300 ml/10 fl oz double cream

1 If you are making the crème fraîche, begin at least a day ahead. Put the buttermilk in a preserving jar or a jar with a screw top. Add the cream, securely close and shake to blend. Leave to set at warm room temperature for 6–8 hours, then refrigerate for at least 8 hours and up to 4 days. It will develop a slightly tangy flavour. Lightly beat before using.

2 To toast the almonds for the decoration, place in a dry frying pan over a medium heat and stir until lightly browned. Take care that they do not burn. Immediately tip the almonds out of the pan. Set aside.

3 To make the orange-blossom cream, put the crème fraîche in a small bowl and stir in 4 tablespoons orange-blossom water, with the honey and the orange rind. Taste and add a little extra orange-blossom water if necessary, and sweeten with a little more honey, if liked.

4 To serve, cut the stems off the figs, but do not peel them. Stand the figs upright with the pointed end upwards. Cut each into quarters without cutting all the way through, so you can open them out into attractive 'flowers'.

5 If you are using fig leaves, place one in the centre of each serving plate. Arrange 2 figs on top of each leaf, and spoon a small amount of the orange-flavoured cream alongside them. Sprinkle the cream with the toasted flaked almonds if desired, just before serving.

Creamy Fruit Parfait

On the tiny Greek island of Kythera, this luscious combination of summer fruits and yogurt is served at tavernas, as well as in homes.

NUTRITIONAL INFORMATION

Calories . . . . . . 261 Sugars 17g
Protein . . . . 10g Fat 18g
Carbohydrate . . 17g Saturates 7g

15 mins 0 mins

SERVES 4–6

INGREDIENTS

225 g/8 oz fresh, juicy cherries

2 large peaches

2 large apricots

700 ml/1¼ pints Greek strained yogurt, or natural thick yogurt

60 g/2¼ oz walnut halves

2 tbsp flower-scented honey, or to taste

fresh redcurrants or berries, to decorate (optional)

1 To prepare the fruit, use a cherry or olive stoner to remove the cherry stones. Cut each cherry in half. Cut the peaches and apricots in half lengthways and remove the stones, then chop the flesh of the fruit finely.

2 Place the finely chopped cherries, peaches and apricots in a bowl and gently stir together.

3 Spoon one-third of the yogurt into individual glass dishes or a glass serving bowl. Top with half the fruit.

4 Repeat with another layer of yogurt and fruit, then top the layers with the remaining yogurt.

5 Place the walnuts in a small food processor and pulse until chopped but not finely ground. Sprinkle the walnuts over the yogurt.

6 Drizzle the honey over the nuts and yogurt. Cover the bowl with cling film and chill for at least 1 hour. Decorate the bowl with a small bunch of redcurrants, if using, just before serving.

VARIATIONS

Vary the fruit to whatever is best in the market. Berries, figs, seedless grapes and melons are also delicious in this simple dessert. In winter, replace the fresh fruits with a compote of soaked mixed dried fruits.

Lemon Rice Pudding

Rice is a staple ingredient in many Mediterranean kitchens. Here it is transformed into a creamy, family-style dessert.

NUTRITIONAL INFORMATION

Calories	332	Sugars	22g
Protein	11g	Fat	10g
Carbohydrate	52g	Saturates	3g

🍲 🍲

🍱 10 mins, plus 1hr chilling   ⏱ 25 mins

SERVES 4

INGREDIENTS

1 tsp cornflour

850 ml/1½ pints milk

125 g/4½ oz short-grain rice

2 tbsp sugar, or 1 tbsp honey, to taste

finely grated rind of 1 large lemon

freshly squeezed lemon juice, to taste

50 g/1¾ oz shelled pistachio nuts

1 Place the cornflour in a small bowl and gradually stir in 2 tablespoons of the milk. Rinse a pan with cold water and do not dry it out.

2 Pour the remaining milk and the cornflour mixture in the pan over a medium–high heat. Stirring occasionally, heat until just simmering. Do not boil.

3 Stir in the rice, lower the heat and continue stirring for 20 minutes, or until all but most of the excess liquid has evaporated and the rice is tender.

4 Remove from the heat and pour into a heatproof bowl. Stir in the lemon rind and sugar to taste. If a slightly tarter flavour is required, stir in freshly squeezed lemon juice. Allow to cool completely.

5 Tightly cover the cool rice with a sheet of cling film and chill in the refrigerator for at least one hour – the colder the rice is when served, the better it tastes with fresh fruit.

6 Meanwhile, using a sharp knife, finely chop the pistachio nuts. To serve, spoon the rice pudding into individual bowls and sprinkle with the chopped nuts.

COOK'S TIP

It is important to rinse the saucepan in Step 1 to prevent the milk scorching on the sides and on the base of the pan.

Lemon Granita

Soft and granular, this iced dessert has a sharp, flavour, which is refreshing and ideal for rounding off any rich meal.

NUTRITIONAL INFORMATION

Calories	 78	Sugars	. . . . 20g
Protein	. . . . 1g	Fat	. . . . 0g
Carbohydrate	. . 20g	Saturates	. . . . . . 0g

15 mins, plus 5 hrs freezing

10 mins

SERVES 4–6

INGREDIENTS

4 large unwaxed lemons

100 g/3½ oz caster sugar

700 ml/1¼ pints water

mint sprigs to decorate

1 Pare 6 strips of rind from one lemon, then finely grate the remaining rind from the remaining lemons, being very careful not to remove any bitter white pith.

2 Roll the lemons back and forth on the work surface, pressing down firmly. Cut each in half and squeeze 125 ml/4 fl oz juice. Add the grated rind to the juice. Set aside.

VARIATION

Lemon-scented fresh herbs add a unique and unexpected flavour. Add 4 small sprigs lemon balm or 2 sprigs lemon thyme to the syrup in Step 3. Remove with the pared rind in Step 4. Or stir ½ tablespoon finely chopped lemon thyme into the mixture in Step 4.

3 Put the pared strips of lemon rind, sugar and water in a saucepan and stir over a low heat to dissolve the sugar. Increase the heat and boil for 4 minutes, without stirring. Use a wet pastry brush to brush down any spatters on the side of the pan. Remove from the heat, pour into a non-metallic bowl and leave to cool.

4 Remove the strips of rind. Stir in the grated rind and juice. Transfer to a shallow metal container, cover and freeze for at least 5 hours, until frozen.

5 Chill serving bowls 30 minutes before serving. To serve, invert the container on to a chopping board. Rinse a cloth in very hot water, wring it out, then rub on the bottom of the container for 15 seconds. Give the container a shake and the mixture should fall out. If not, repeat.

6 Use a knife to break up the granita and transfer to a food processor. Quickly process until it becomes granular. Serve at once in the chilled bowls (or in scooped-out lemons). Decorate with mint.

Espresso Granita

Enjoy this crunchy, coffee granita as a cooling mid-morning snack or as a light dessert after a substantial meal.

NUTRITIONAL INFORMATION

Calories	 133	Sugars	.... 35g
Protein	.... 0g	Fat	.... 0g
Carbohydrate	.. 35g	Saturates	...... 0g

🍧 🍧

10 mins, plus 5 hours freezing   ⏱ 10 mins

SERVES 4–6

INGREDIENTS

200 g/7 oz caster sugar

600 ml/1 pint water

½ tsp vanilla essence

600 ml/1 pint very strong espresso coffee, chilled

fresh mint, to garnish

1 Put the sugar in a saucepan with the water and stir over a low heat to dissolve the sugar. Increase the heat and boil for 4 minutes, without stirring. Use a wet pastry brush to brush down any spatters on the side of the pan.

2 Remove the pan from the heat and pour the syrup into a heat-proof non-metallic bowl. Sit the bowl in the kitchen sink filled with iced water to speed up the cooling process. Stir in the vanilla and coffee and leave until completely cool.

3 Transfer to a shallow metal container, cover and freeze for at least 5 hours, until frozen. The granita can be kept in the freezer for up to 3 months.

4 Thirty minutes before serving, chill serving bowls in the refrigerator.

5 To serve, invert the container on to a chopping board. Rinse a cloth in very hot water, wring it out, then rub on the bottom of the container for 15 seconds. Give the container a sharp shake and the mixture should fall out. If not, repeat.

6 Use a knife to break up the granita and transfer to a food processor. Quickly process until it becomes grainy and crunchy. Serve at once in the chilled bowls, decorated with mint.

COOK'S TIP

A very dark, fruit-flavoured espresso is the only choice for this Italian speciality. Otherwise, the flavour will be marred in the freezing process.

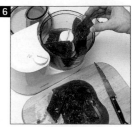

This is a Parragon Book
First published in 2001

Parragon
Queen Street House
4 Queen Street
Bath BA1 1HE, UK

ISBN: 0-75255-078-0

Printed in Italy

NOTE

This book uses metric and imperial measurements. Follow the same units
of measurement throughout; do not mix metric and imperial.
All spoon measurements are level: teaspoons are assumed to be 5 ml, and
tablespoons are assumed to be 15 ml. Unless otherwise stated,
milk is assumed to be full fat, eggs and individual vegetables such as potatoes
are medium, and pepper is freshly ground black pepper.

The nutritional information provided for each recipe is per serving or per person.
Optional ingredients, variations or serving suggestions have
not been included in the calculations. The times given for each recipe are an approximate
guide only because the preparation times may differ according to the techniques used by
different people and the cooking times may vary as a result of the type of oven used.

Recipes using raw or very lightly cooked eggs should be
avoided by infants, the elderly, pregnant women, convalescents,
and anyone suffering from an illness.

The publisher would like to thank
Steamer Trading Cookshop, Lewes, East Sussex, for the kind loan of props.